GLAZES
FOR
SPECIAL
EFFECTS

Fluted crystal glaze piece illustrating Commercial Frit Glaze #1 colored with copper oxide.

GLAZES
FOR
SPECIAL
EFFECTS

BY HERBERT H. SANDERS

WATSON-GUPTILL PUBLICATIONS/NEW YORK

Copyright © 1974 by Watson-Guptill Publications

First published 1974 in the United States and Canada by Watson-Guptill Publications,
a division of Billboard Publications, Inc.,
One Astor Plaza, New York, N.Y. 10036

Manufactured in U.S.A.

Library of Congress Cataloging in Publication Data
Sanders, Herbert H
    Glazes for special effects.
    Bibliography: p.
    1. Glazes. I. Title.
TT922.S26   738.1'44   74-6126
ISBN 0-8230-2134-3

First Printing, 1974

To my students

CONTENTS

Acknowledgments

The author wishes to acknowledge his gratitude to the many students and friends who contributed to this book. Many students at the California State University at San Jose as well as professors of ceramics contributed examples of processes and completed ware. I have tried to include the name of the artist along with the photographed example.

All photos are by John Bobeda, except the ones on page 81, which are by Fred Gaeden; photos of crystal pieces glazed with commercial frits are by Hugh Aanonsen; the raku demonstration photos are by Russell Gamble.

Where glaze compositions are presented, they were provided by the individual whose name accompanies the composition. Other glaze compositions were provided by the author.

Any acknowledgments would be incomplete without mention of the testing and firing of glazes carried out by Robert E. Johnson.

Introduction

The glazes discussed in this book are ones about which it is difficult to find information, and for that reason if for no other they will be of interest to every potter. The information on glazes presented here is information which endures. It does not go out of style. Information is presented on crystalline glazes, on copper red glazes, on glazes from wood ash and plant ash, on luster glazes, and on raku ware. All these chapters are particularly pertinent today when there is a revival of interest in all kinds of glazing. And because potters interested in ceramics are realizing that glazing is a part of the whole field in which they are working, this interest shows indications of growing very rapidly. Any knowledge of ceramics is incomplete without some knowledge of glazes.

Crystals

Before you can use crystalline, or crystal, glazes effectively, you should understand how and why crystals form in a glaze. Although what actually happens is not fully known and more scientific observation and investigation is necessary in this area, the following is what chemists now believe takes place as crystals form.

Basic Structure of Glass

As you know, a glaze is a glass. It is our present understanding that the basic structural unit of glass is a tetrahedral molecule in which there is a linkage of one silica atom to four oxygen atoms. These basic units are in turn attached to one another to form a three-dimensional, noncrystalline network, or lattice structure, which is continuous but whose units are spaced at random intervals. It is thought that this network is dynamic—that is, the bonds that form the network are constantly forming, disintegrating, and re-forming. Think, then, of the basic unit structure of glass as a three-dimensional fishnet of non-uniform mesh composed of silica and oxygen.

The skeletal unit of glass therefore becomes a tetrahedral coordination of the glass-former silica with oxygen. The spaces within the network are filled or partly filled by stabilizing elements that affect the physical properties of glass. The stabilizers most commonly present in crystalline glazes are sodium, potassium, magnesium, zinc, lithium, and sometimes calcium. These elements in turn combine with oxygen and form groups within the glassy matrix.

Function of the Lattice Structure in Glazes

The lattice structure of the glaze plays an important role in its performance on the clay product. Internal friction of the atoms individually or in collective masses is responsible for viscosity in a glaze. The more continuous the lattice structure, the less freely the glaze will flow. It follows then that the lattice is weakened when extended or broken and the glaze becomes fluid; with increased lattice breakdown, the glaze may flow from the piece.

How Crystals Form

In the development of crystalline glazes, it is necessary to heat the glaze to the point at which the lattice structure is radically stretched or broken down sufficiently for the glaze to become fluid. This fluid condition of the glaze matrix permits the oxide of silica and the filler oxides of zinc, sodium,

Crystals have many shapes. Here the crystal pattern is a cluster of flowers.

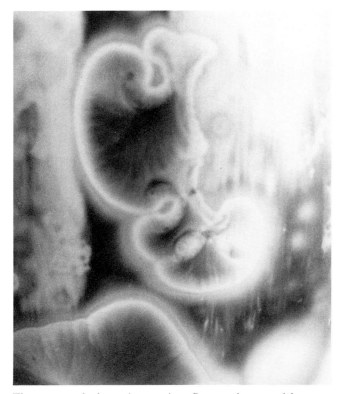

These crystals have interesting flower shapes with many secondary crystals in the background.

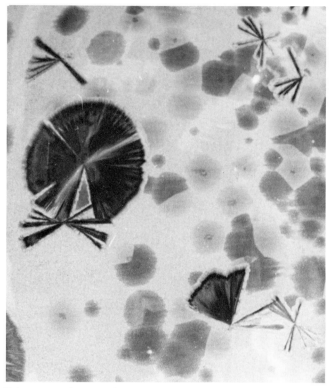

Primary and secondary crystals, as well as circular spots, may or may not be crystalline in origin.

A combination of primary and secondary crystals.

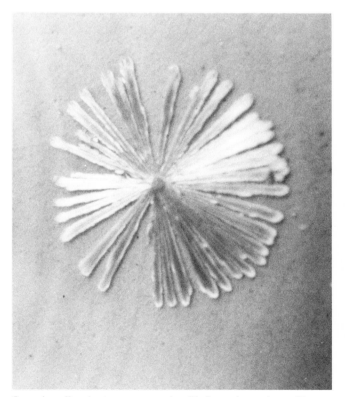

Here an umbel of flowers shows the basic crystal structure.

Occasionally, just one crystal will form in a glaze. Here a sunburst dominates with very small crystals in the background.

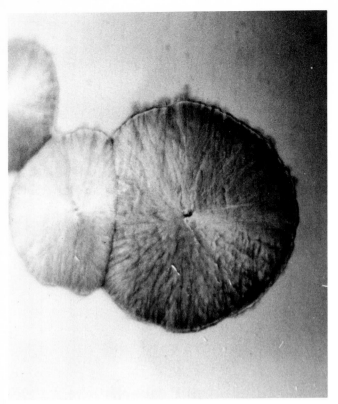

Solid circular crystal forms may occur.

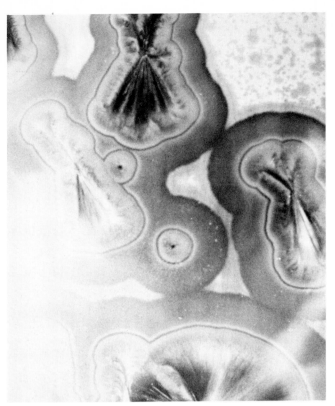

These crystals form fan shapes with halos as well as rods and circular forms, with secondary crystals in the background.

A seeded glaze may produce large crystals in the seeded area, as well as smaller crystals where there has been no seeding. The smaller crystals result from the crystal glaze alone.

The rod is the basic structural unit for this type of crystal which produces a mixture of rods, sunbursts, and pinwheels.

Crystal patterns may be very subtle and elusive.

potassium, magnesium, and lithium (whichever of these may be present in the specific glaze composition) to move freely within the glaze. When the kiln is turned off, thermal motion within the glaze diminishes. During this period, the bonds that form the lattice are constantly forming and disintegrating. At some point in the cooling process, the re-forming bonds will, on the basis of chance, combine to form perfect unit cells of the crystallizing agent, which in turn provide a nucleus around which crystals may form. When the lattice is sufficiently broken down, the unit cells are dispersed, the proper atoms are attached, and the crystal pattern develops.

What Crystals Are

A crystal glaze is a devitrified glaze, which means that if a crystal-forming agent were not present in the glaze, the excess silica would form microscopic crystals that would look like scum on the surface of the glaze. By providing an excessive amount of zinc oxide in a glaze composition, we take advantage of the tendency toward devitrification to create crystal-forming groups. Zinc oxide and silica have an affinity for each other and tend to combine to form the natural mineral Willemite, which is native zinc orthosilicate ($Zn_2 \cdot SiO_4$) or ($2 ZnO \cdot SiO_2$). The crystal patterns seen on pots are composed of zinc orthosilicate crystals. (It is not necessary for you to understand this information in order to have the glazes in this book work for you.)

Secondary Crystals

Among the various glaze compositions in which zinc orthosilicate crystals form, there are some that also produce secondary crystals. Compared with the zinc silicate crystal patterns, the secondary crystal forms are quite small. To date, the largest secondary crystal observed has been approximately 1/4″ in diameter, and secondary crystals are usually much smaller than that. (Although circular spots 1/2″ or more in diameter have been observed in some glazes, it is not known whether or not these were crystalline in nature.)

There may be only one form of secondary crystal present in a particular glaze; at other times or in other glaze compositions, as many as three or four secondary forms may be seen. Some of these forms appear to be solid rectangles about 1/8″ long and are usually darker than the other colors in the glaze. Another form that frequently occurs is the circular dot, which may be darker or lighter than the background color. Dots range from pinpoint size to 1/8″ in diameter. Triangular, solid color forms occur less frequently than the rectangles and dots. These are always about 1/8″ maximum measurement and quite dark in color, and very few have been found in the transparent, colored background of glazes.

A fourth type of secondary crystal is the transparent, colorless, perfectly formed, roughly circular crystal that may appear on the surface of the glaze. When these forms occur, they are prolific and vary in diameter from 1/16″ to 3/16″. They are not always apparent when the piece is looked at directly but sometimes become visible when the piece is viewed at an angle. For this reason, these crystals have been called "ghosts." The ghost crystal seems to occur most often in glazes in which cobalt has been used as a coloring oxide. An interesting feature of the ghosts is that they form indiscriminately — they may appear on a transparent background or on areas where large zinc crystals are submerged in the glaze.

Finally, there is a type of secondary crystal that appears as a white fleck about 1/16″ in diameter in glazes that are colored by nickel. These appear as irregular, somewhat fuzzy circles, not perfect circles like the ghost crystals. These white flecks are usually distributed very evenly throughout the amber colored background.

What causes secondary crystals to develop is unknown. However, it is known that a rather prolonged cooling period is necessary for the development of all kinds of crystal growth, with the exception of chrome red crystals. The pieces displaying the secondary crystals mentioned here were fired in a naturally slow-cooling kiln, held at approximately 2085°F. (1140°C.) for three hours during the cooling process.

Questions about Secondary Crystals

Since secondary crystals create additional interesting effects in crystal glazes, it would be useful to know how and why they form. The following questions still need to be answered in regard to these crystals. First, are they simply a different form of zinc orthosilicate crystals? If so, why the difference in color or the occasional complete lack of color? Second, are secondary crystals a completely different compound of silica in combination with something other than zinc? Does some material dissolve from the ceramic body, combine with silica, and crystallize? Or do these compounds crystallize from the materials present in the glaze itself? If they are direct products of the glaze, why do they not always form? When do they form? Do they form before or after the zinc crystals have formed? There is another possible explanation for sec-

ondary crystals: that they result from the use of certain coloring oxides. However, this hardly seems likely, since they never seem to be the same color as the other crystals or the background. And the final question is probably the most interesting: why do secondary crystals develop in one firing of a specific glaze and not in another firing? None of these questions has as yet been answered.

Shapes of Crystals

The shapes of crystals and crystal patterns are unpredictable. The shape of a crystal in a specific glaze composition varies from one firing to another; perfect sunburst crystals may result from firing in one kiln, while flower shapes occur in another. Some of the shapes you can expect are: sunbursts, flower forms, butterfly forms, rods, fans, circles, battle-axe forms, rods which fan out at the ends, and nearly anything else imaginable. There does not seem to be any way in which you can plan or control what will happen. Although there does seem to be a minor relationship between crystal forms and holding temperature, the extent of this has not been definitely determined. Don't become overly attached to the idea of having a certain crystal form on a specific piece; crystal forming does not work that way.

Quite frequently, four or five crystal forms will appear on one piece. At other times, all the crystals will be of one form. Regardless of which form or forms develop, they are always interesting.

Crystal Patterns

Crystal arrangements or patterns are also something beyond the potter's control. Crystals sometimes cluster together in one place, sometimes they form very interesting scattered patterns or groupings, while at still other times they cover the entire surface of the piece. There are also times when only one or two crystals, and occasionally none at all, will form.

Seeding Crystals

When you take your first piece from the kiln and find no crystals in the glaze — and this will happen — this is the time to try seeding. The idea behind this comparatively unexplored field is to artificially provide a nucleus around which a crystal will develop. However, since you will be working with crystalline glazes, it may be difficult to keep crystals from forming in areas you have not seeded. The problem is to find a glaze that produces no crystals after being fired in a manner that should

The interesting placement of primary crystals, secondary crystals, and spots is dramatically illustrated on this covered jar.

cause it to produce crystals — a glaze in which all the unit cells that should have acted as crystal-forming nuclei have instead disintegrated in the glaze.

Even in such a glaze, all the atoms of the crystallizing agent will still be present. Therefore, we cannot be sure that unit cells will *not* form when the glaze is reheated, although experience indicates that most crystalline glazes that do not produce crystals in the first firing are even less likely to produce them when fired again.

Materials for Seeding Crystals

In his article, "Control of Crystalline Glazes" (see Bibliography), F. H. Norton recommends applying a nucleus-forming material to the point in the glaze where crystals are desired. He has seeded crystals successfully with sodium carbonate, calcium carbonate, zinc oxide, and silica. I have been successful using the raw composition of zinc orthosilciate as the seeding agent. This is composed of 162 parts by weight of zinc oxide and 60 parts by weight of silica, wet-ground thoroughly with either a mortar and pestle or a ball mill, using a medium-thin solution of gum tragacanth instead of water.

I have also used this composition as an under-glaze coat in isolated areas on the biscuit. However, although this seeding procedure did work, it was applied under a glaze known to produce crystals consistently, and a few other crystals also formed in the glaze.

Mercuric oxide has also been reported to act as a seeding agent, and while it is expensive, you may find it worth trying if you are interested in the possibilities of seeding.

Procedures for Seeding Crystals. Norton has found that either of the following two procedures is effective in seeding the molten glaze when it is at the growing temperature for crystals.

1. Blow a few particles of the seeding material through a tube onto the hot glaze.

2. Pick up a particle of seeding material on a steel point and apply it to the hot glaze while the piece is in the kiln.

3. You may also use the tip of a well-pointed brush to pick up and apply the material to the glaze after the piece has been removed from the kiln, then simply re-fire the piece.

Crystal patterns may be very dramatic, as in this glaze that displays Willemite crystals under shortwave black light.

Crystalline Glazes

In this chapter I will discuss the crystalline glazes that are based upon zinc orthosilicate crystals. Within this category, there are two kinds of zinc orthosilicate glazes — those that are applied raw, or unfritted, and those that contain one or more frits. As you experiment with crystalline glazes, you will probably find that those composed of frits you make yourself offer the greatest latitude for creating interesting crystal patterns and effects.

Clay Bodies for Crystalline Glazes

Before we study specific crystalline glazes, we should consider the clay bodies upon which the glazes are to be used. Each body composition has its own particular effect on crystal formation in the glaze. A single glaze composition can result in a highly glossy crystalline glaze on one body, a matte glaze with crystals on another, and a very fluid glaze completely without crystals on a third.

Crystalline glazes work on both stoneware and porcelain bodies. Therefore, your first decision must be between these two types of clay. If you are accustomed to working with earthenware, or if you have been using a body containing grog, either of these bodies will mean quite a change for you. The body you use for crystalline glazes should be very smooth, without grog or sand. A coarse-textured clay such as earthenware vies with the crystals for attention, thus detracting from your final product. A good stoneware or porcelain body, which matures at cone 10 or 12, will do nicely.

The gray or tan color of stoneware will somewhat influence the general effect of your glazes. Since most crystalline glazes are transparent and glossy, you will get a much more colorful and sparkling result if you use a porcelain body. In fact, a specific crystalline glaze may even change color when used on two different porcelain bodies, and it may be to your advantage to run a series of tests on a number of body compositions before making a final decision as to which one to use.

Preparing Porcelain Bodies

The preparation of a porcelain body requires some labor, but it is time well spent. First, weigh out all your materials, then screen them together twice through a 60-mesh screen. This is a very important part of the preparation; if the materials are not thoroughly mixed, lumps will occur in the body when water is added. When the materials are thoroughly mixed together, sift them into a tub two-thirds full of water. There should be at least one inch of water above the materials in the tub. Permit the tub of materials to set overnight.

Next day, stir with a smooth (no slivers, please) wooden paddle until you have a creamy slip. Stir it two or three times, permitting the materials to settle for five or six hours between stirrings. After the slip seems thoroughly stirred, let it set for several days until the excess water evaporates. When the body has thickened, place it on plaster evaporating bats until it reaches the right consistency. Then wedge it, place it in strong plastic bags, and store it in a dark place for aging. The longer it ages, the better, as its workability improves with age. Never ball-mill a porcelain body. Ball-milling will make it smoother but will also round off the edges of the grains of material, making the particles smooth as marbles. When you try to throw a milled body, the "marbles" will slide over one another and end up at the bottom of the piece. Milling can make porcelain almost impossible to throw. Throw with thick slip, not water, to avoid S-shaped cracks in the bottom of your pieces.

Using Porcelain

Once you have decided on a specific body composition, use it consistently, particularly if you are using porcelain. Each porcelain body has its own characteristics. It takes time to become accustomed to the throwing qualities of a particular porcelain body. After you have used a specific porcelain for a year or two, you will know what to expect from it; the longer you use it, the easier it will be to use. If you change bodies, it may be another year before you feel comfortable with the throwing characteristics of the new body.

There is a general feeling that because porcelain is translucent in thin sections, it should always be thrown very thin. However, this is not always true. If thrown too thin, porcelain often warps or distorts when fired to maturity. Any porcelain piece thrown should have a substantial wall. Like any well-thrown form, its wall thickness should be as uniform as possible. The wall near the base should be somewhat thicker than the higher sections to support the weight of the wall above. Remember also that your purpose in using crystalline glazes is not to show the translucence of the body but to provide a white background for crystal formations.

Porcelain Body Compositions

If you are using a stoneware body, you can save yourself much time by using one of the many good ones on the market. There are also one or two fairly good porcelain bodies on the market. If you find one you like that is workable, use it. However, you will probably want to mix your own porcelain body, so here are a few compositions for you to try. The names and addresses of suppliers from whom you can obtain the ingredients listed here, as well as those listed for the glaze compositions, throughout the rest of this book, are located in the Suppliers List. "Pbw" after the material amount means parts by weight throughout the book.

Body Composition #1 (cone 9 – 10)

Del Monte feldspar (200 mesh)	40%
Del Monte silica (200 mesh)	14%
Spinks C&C ball clay	27%
Ione kaolin	19%

Note: This body is difficult to throw. It must be quite stiff to stand up in throwing pieces of any size. (For smaller pieces it is more easily worked.) Crystalline glazes react remarkably well on it.

Body Composition #2 (cone 9 – 12)

Talc	51.72%
Imperial ball clay	21.55%
Victoria ball clay	14.37%
Plastic Vitrox	12.36%

Note: There could be some argument as to whether this is a true porcelain body composition. However, it works remarkably well with crystalline glazes. For porcelain, this body has average throwing qualities.

Body Composition #3 (cone 9 – 10)

Del Monte feldspar	320 pbw
Del Monte silica (200 mesh)	112
Tennessee ball clay	216
Edgar plastic kaolin	152
Bentonite	40

Note: This is a remarkable throwing body, but it must not be fired above cone 10 or it will begin to bloat.

Body Composition #4 (cone 9 – 12)

Kingman feldspar	22.00%
Edgar plastic kaolin	43.50%
Silica	21.50%
Nepheline syenite	6.70%
Bentonite	3.00%
Kentucky ball clay #4	3.30%

Note: This probably is the best of the porcelain bodies listed here. It throws well, has good color, and works well with crystalline glazes.

Body Composition #5 (cone 9 – 12)

Keystone feldspar	21 pbw
Edgar plastic kaolin	42
Silica	21
Kentucky ball clay #4	8
Bentonite	4

Note: This body has worked very well for small pieces.

Do not heat porcelain pieces rapidly until they are already well above red heat; do not cool them rapidly until they are well below red heat. Remember also not to take porcelain pieces from the kiln until they are cool enough to handle without gloves — cold shock may cause porcelain to split.

After biscuit firing, the surface of porcelain often remains powdery. Wash the piece well to remove the dust and dry it well before glazing. Many potters recommend a hard biscuit fire — cone 02 is not too high for biscuit fire of porcelain to be used with crystalline glazes.

Raw Zinc Silicate Glaze Compositions

Zinc silicate crystals result in two types of glazes: those composed of raw, unfritted material, and those which are fritted. We will consider the unfritted glazes first.

The reason that raw, unfritted zinc crystal glazes are so rare is that most of them contain some materials that are soluble in water. This means that when they are mixed with water they must be used immediately. You should not leave a raw crystalline glaze in the jar unused; the longer the glaze sets, the more materials will go into solution. When finally used, a large percentage of the materials will soak into the pores of the body, changing both the body and glaze composition.

The G.S. glaze listed below is an exception because it contains no soluble materials. To use the two E.W.S. glazes, weigh out the materials, mix them with water, screen them through a 60-mesh screen, and use them at once.

Raw Crystalline Glaze E.W.S. #1 (cone 13 – 15)

Powdered potassium carbonate	32 pbw
Whiting	9
Soda ash	5
Zinc oxide	47
Edgar plastic kaolin	21
Silica	83
Titanium dioxide	2
Ferro frit #5301	40

*Crystals may develop as an overall pattern,
as they have on this piece glazed
with "K" brand sodium silicate.*

Note: When you use zinc oxide raw, or in an unfritted glaze, use a calcined zinc, such as that found in St. Joe #44 zinc oxide.

Raw Crystalline Glaze E.W.S. #2 (cone 13 –15)

Powdered potassium carbonate	14 pbw
Zinc oxide	50
Soda ash	30
Alumina	20
Silica	96
Calcined borax	10

Raw Crystalline Glaze G.S. #3 (cone 8 – 10)

Kingman feldspar	75 pbw
Colemanite	40
Zinc oxide	35

Note: This glaze is comparatively untried. It is known that it will work, but it could stand considerable experimentation.

There is no specific firing schedule for the above glazes. However, you should try firing them to maturing temperature, then cooling to 2085°F. (1140°C.) and holding there for 3 hours.

Raw Sodium Silicate Glaze Compositions

Another group of raw crystalline glazes is made with sodium silicates. These liquid silicate glazes should be brushed on the ware. When sprayed on the piece, they tend to peel off as they dry. Sodium silicate glazes need not be ground, but they should be screened through a 60-mesh screen and used immediately. If they are permitted to set unused, they form a thick scum on the surface and eventually solidify.

Some liquid silicates, either sodium or potassium, are thicker than others. You may need to add a few cubic centimeters of water to the thicker ones to create a consistency for brushing. When you prepare such a glaze, fill the graduated tube you use for measuring the silicate with 5 cc of water and then add it to the glaze. Apply only one coat of the glaze to the piece. When not in use, keep the silicate container tightly sealed.

Liquid Sodium Silicate Glaze (cone 7 – 10)

"K" brand sodium silicate	49.69 cc
Silica	19.46 grams
Zinc oxide	17.95 grams
Titanium oxide	7.94 grams
Water	4.96 cc

Note: This glaze was first developed by H. M. Kraner (see Bibliography.) Fire to cone 7 in 10 to 13 hours, then slowly cool to 1652°F. (900°C.) in 16 to 17 hours. You may also follow this alternate schedule: fire to cone 9 or 10 in 12 hours, cool to 2012°F. (1100°C.) for 3 hours, then cool normally.

Liquid Sodium Silicate Glaze (cone 12)

B. W. Brand sodium silicate	30 cc
Zinc oxide	25 grams
Silica	30 grams
Eureka spar	15 grams
Rutile	5 grams
Manganese carbonate	0.5 grams
Copper carbonate	3 grams
Magnesium carbonate	10 grams

Note: This recipe produces a good brown matte at cone 8 and 9. Excellent crystals result when fired at cone 11. This glaze should be ground for a half hour and sprayed on biscuit.

Liquid Sodium Silicate Glaze (cone 10 – 12)

"N" brand sodium silicate	50 cc
Silica	25 grams
Zinc oxide (St. Joe #44)	25 grams
Titanium oxide	5 grams

Note: Mix up this glaze and paint it directly onto the ware.

Powdered Sodium Silicate Glaze (cone 9 – 11)

SS-65 brand sodium silicate	41.0%
Titanium oxide	11.5%
Zinc oxide	26.0%
Silica	21.5%

Note: If possible, this glaze should be ground for a half hour on a ball mill and then sprayed on the ware. Keep powdered silicate in a tightly sealed container when not in use or it will cake. Caking does not spoil the silicate, but it takes a lot of work to grind it into powder again. There are two additional liquid silicates whose results are very promising, although more work needs to be done with them. These are "RU" brand and "Kasil #1" brand liquid silicates. Correct application and firing are very important in working with the silicates. Try them at different temperatures with prolonged cooling, or hold them between 2000°F. and 2100°F. (1090° and 1150°C.) during cooling.

Line blends or triaxial blends (the mixing of glazes by percentage to achieve a new glaze) of the compositions listed above should be rewarding.

*A few large and many small crystals
are distributed on this piece
glazed with Sodium Silicate Glaze SS-65.*

Reasons for Fritting a Glaze

There are several reasons for fritting a glaze, and they cover a rather broad area in respect to glazes. A glaze may be fritted for the following reasons:

To make a poisonous glaze nonpoisonous. Several materials used by the potter, such as lead, barium, and cadmium, are poisonous to humans. The worst offender is probably lead. When fused into a glass with the proper ceramic materials, then powdered and used as a frit, these poisonous materials are no longer poisonous, since they have become insoluble. Fritting poisonous materials does not absolutely guarantee that the glazes made from the frit will not be poisonous, and you should make sure that any glazes containing lead, either raw or fritted, are tested for lead solubility before being used on food or drink containers.

To make soluble materials insoluble. When made into a glaze slip, many materials dissolve in the water used. These include sodium carbonate, potassium carbonate, borax, and boric acid. When these materials are used in glazes in the raw state, they dissolve and soak into the body of the biscuited ware, changing the composition of the body and the glaze. When they are fritted with the appropriate ceramic materials before being used in the glaze, they become insoluble in water and remain in the glaze.

To lower the fusion or melting point of the glaze. Each glaze material has its own fusion point. Some materials, such as barium compounds, are quite resistant to fusing when used raw. In an unfritted glaze, the materials with the lowest fusion point melt first and gradually, over a prolonged period of time, bring the other glaze materials into solution. When the materials are first fritted together, all particles of the frit melt at one temperature – the melting temperature of the frit, which is lower than the point of complete fusion for the unfritted glaze.

To eliminate blisters and bubbles from the glaze. When used raw, many materials contain water in chemical combination. Borax and feldspar are two such materials. Other materials contain carbon, excess oxygen, and sometimes nitrogen and hydrogen. When the materials melt, these elements are eliminated in the form of steam or gas bubbles that may remain in the molten glaze or escape through the glaze coat to cause blisters. During the fritting process, the steam and gases are eliminated from the glaze, and a smooth, uniform melt without blisters or bubbles is assured.

To achieve results not possible by using any other means. This is probably the most important reason for fritting glazes. Crystals usually do not result when the materials used to produce a crystalline frit — soda ash, potassium carbonate, zinc oxide, and silica — are used as raw, rather than fritted, materials. When these same materials are first fritted in the proper proportions and the glaze is then properly fired, large, interesting crystals will inevitably result. There are several reasons for this, the most important of which is the solubility of the sodium and potassium compounds used — when fritted, they become insoluble. The second reason is the nature of the materials themselves; they work one way when fritted, another when unfritted. The third factor is the difference between the firing temperatures required for the same materials fritted and unfritted; much higher temperatures are needed to fire unfritted materials. Also, the body is affected by unfritted materials in a different way than it is by fritted materials; although both fritted and unfritted materials take some of the body into solution, fritted materials take less of it than do unfritted materials. Occasionally, if the raw materials can be fired to high enough temperatures and cooled slowly enough, needle crystals will form. If you wish to try this — which means that you will be using an unfritted composition as a glaze — first biscuit your ware to maturity and then apply the glaze and fire it. You will probably need to fire several cones above the maturing temperature.

Preparing Commercial-Frit Glazes

The commercial-frit glaze compositions listed a bit further on need no milling. To prepare them, mix the materials with just enough water to pass them through a 60-mesh screen. Although some potters recommend using a 100-mesh lawn for screening crystalline glazes, I prefer the 60-mesh screen; this coarser mesh often results in a glaze that contains streaks, speckles, and mottlings of background color that do not occur with a 100-mesh screen. In any case, after screening the materials, add gum tragacanth solution the consistency of molasses, two tablespoons to a pint of glaze. Since crystalline glazes should be sprayed on the piece, add just enough water to create a spraying consistency. Pouring is not recommended for these or any crystalline glazes, as the irregularities that result may destroy already-formed crystals as the glaze flows, and dipping requires too large a quantity of glaze. Less than 1/16″ of glaze should be an adequate coat; the glaze coating should be tapered to about 1/32″ toward the bottom of the piece.

Making Gum Tragacanth Solutions

Since gum tragacanth is used to prepare many glaze compositions, this is a good time for you to learn how to make it. Once you've made a gum tragacanth solution, you can keep it on hand for use whenever it is needed. You should begin by soaking 25 grams of powdered gum tragacanth in 100 cubic centimeters of alcohol for five minutes. Be sure the pan is dry before you put either the gum powder or the alcohol into it, or lumps will occur in the solution. Stir the gum and alcohol for about five minutes. You will notice that the grains of powder lose some of their sharp edges. Then turn the water faucet to a smooth, medium flow, place the pan with the gum and alcohol under the running water, and stir the mixture vigorously. Try to stir the entire mixture at once, cleaning the sides of the bowl as you stir. Keep adding water and stirring until the solution reaches the consistency of thin custard or molasses.

You should have about 1/3 gallon of solution. Pour it into a clean glass gallon jug or plastic gallon container, add about eight or ten drops of oil of cloves, shake it vigorously, and replace the cap on the jug. Oil of cloves stops bacterial growth and prevents the gum from souring. The solution can then be stored for later use.

Firing Commercial-Frit Glazes

For the benefit of those who have never worked with crystalline glazes, the firing procedure for two different kilns is presented here. My own firing experience indicates that reduction tends to work against crystal formation; although I have heard reports of crystals developed in a reducing atmosphere, I have had no experience with them. Therefore, I fire my crystal glazes only in electric kilns, and both kiln procedures listed here are for electric kilns.

Procedure A. For a 55-ampere electric Marshall Craft top-loading kiln, 18″ x 18″ x 18″. The kiln is constructed of 2600°F. (about 1440°C.) insulating brick and has Kanthal A elements. It has five 7-step controls and a Leslie Ceramic Co. pyrometer.

1. Set all switches on low or Step 1 for 1/2 hour.

2. Set all switches on high or step 7 until cone 10 down.

3. Turn all switches off until kiln is cooled to 2012°F. (1100°C.).

4. Set all switches on medium or step 4 for 3½ hours, holding kiln at 2012°F. (1100°C.) for that period.

5. Turn all switches off. Allow kiln to cool.

Procedure B. For an Alpine Globar electric kiln, Model EFG-3, with a maximum operating temperature of 3000°F. (about 1650°C.).

1. Set kiln on low or Step 1 (room temperature to 280°F., 140°C.) for 1 hour.

2. Set kiln on medium or Step 2 (280° to 800°F., 140°C. to 430°C.) for 1 hour.

3. Set kiln on high or Step 3 for 6½ hours until cone 10 down.

4. Turn off kiln for 45 minutes. Allow kiln to cool to 2000°F. (about 1100°C.).

5. Set kiln on medium or Step 2 for 3½ hours, holding at 2020°F. (1105°C.) for that period.

Firing crystalline glazes is similar in some ways to firing the copper reduction glazes described in a later chapter. These similarities primarily consist of the unpredictable nature of the results and the possible need for adjustment of the firing schedule. Do not hesitate to fire a cone or two higher than suggested here, or to experiment with various holding temperatures. Your kiln may require a different schedule than either of those given here.

Commercial-Frit Glaze Compositions

Several years of research with commercial frits have resulted in a number of satisfactory glaze compositions, which include the following:

Crystalline Glaze #1 (cone 10 – 12)

Pemco frit #P 283	68.42 pbw
Zinc oxide (St. Joe #44)	24.13
Silica	7.45

Note: This glaze works well with all coloring oxides except chromium. It is an excellent, dependable glaze from cone 10 to 12.

Crystalline Glaze #3 (cone 10)

Ferro frit #3110	52.00 pbw
Zinc oxide (St. Joe #44)	24.34
Silica	23.66

Note: Best color results with cobalt carbonate, manganese oxide, and copper carbonate.

Crystalline Glaze #4 (cone 10)

Ferro frit #3124	50.85 pbw
Zinc oxide (St. Joe #44)	22.32
Silica	26.83

*This piece shows a glaze made
from a combination of crystal frits.*

Note: Good color results from the use of copper carbonate, manganese oxide, iron oxide, and nickel oxide. Nickel is considered to produce superior results.

Crystalline Glaze #6 (cone 10 – 11)

Ferro frit #3134	15.45 pbw
Pemco frit #P 283	39.15
Zinc oxide (St. Joe #44)	23.77
Silica	21.63

Note: A low fluidity glaze. Good colors result with copper carbonate, manganese oxide, iron oxide, nickel oxide, sodium uranate, and cobalt carbonate.

Crystalline Glaze #12 (cone 10)

O. Hommel frit #K3	50.78 pbw
Zinc oxide (St. Joe #44)	20.70
Silica	28.52

Note: Quite fluid glaze. Good colors result with copper carbonate, nickel oxide, and cobalt carbonate.

Crystalline Glaze #13 (cone 10)

O. Hommel frit #5	44.73 pbw
Zinc oxide (St. Joe #44)	24.90
Silica	30.37

Note: This glaze does not flow excessively. All coloring oxides are effective with it.

Crystalline Glaze #18 (cone 10)

Pemco frit #P 239	46.33 pbw
Zinc oxide (St. Joe #44)	26.37
Silica	27.30

Note: Quite fluid glaze. Good color reaction with all colorants. Unusual with manganese oxide 3% and copper carbonate 4% in combination.

Crystalline Glaze #19 (cone 10)

Pemco frit #P 757	48.21 pbw
Zinc oxide (St. Joe #44)	19.82
Silica	31.97

Note: Good color reactions. Will blister on occasion unless allowed to flow beyond the foot rim. (See the section on *Preparing Crystalline-Glazed Pieces* for how to avoid damaging kiln shelves with glazes which have run.)

Crystalline Glaze #21 (cone 10)

Pemco frit #P 760	50.42 pbw
Zinc oxide (St. Joe #44)	24.83
Edgar plastic kaolin	1.36
Silica	23.39

Note: Copper carbonate is particularly effective in this glaze.

Crystalline Glaze #28 (cone 10 –13)

Pemco frit #PIN 72	40.20 pbw
Zinc oxide (St. Joe #44)	24.30
Silica	35.50

Note: Most coloring oxides effective in this glaze. Use delicate colors with less than 2% colorants.

Aanonsen & Johnson Crystalline Glaze (cone 8 – 10)

Ferro frit #3110	65 pbw
Zinc oxide (St. Joe #44)	25
Silica	15

Note: Good with all colorants.

Crystalline Glaze #30 (cone 10 – 12)

Western Ceramics Supply Co. Frit #221 – 112	65 pbw
Zinc oxide (St. Joe #44)	25
Silica	15

Note: A new frit, comparatively untried, it is excellent with copper at cone 10 or cone 11 and may also work at a lower cone.

Making Your Own Crystal Frits

Some potters prefer to have more control over the composition of their glazes than commercial frits provide. A commercial frit has to be adapted to a crystal glaze, while a crystal frit is designed exclusively for crystal development. Some crystal frits are designed to be used alone with only coloring oxides added. However, most frits work in combination with others, and occasionally one is designed expressly to be used in combination with others.

While it is laborious, making your own crystal frits can be a lot of fun. By the time you have made two or three different frits, you will see that the possible combinations are unlimited. Of course, if you have or know someone who has a frit furnace, it can be a very simple process. If no frit furnace is available, you can make frits in your kiln.

*Covered jar coated with Crystal
Frit Glaze A-7 with iron oxide.*

Procedure for Making Crystal Frits. To make a frit, you will need a few simple and comparatively inexpensive pieces of equipment. First, you should have a large saggar — you can use a large biscuited stoneware bowl for this. Make the bowl comparatively flat so that you can spread the materials as thin as possible. While not a must, a ball mill will save you hours of work, and an iron mortar and pestle are absolutely necessary.

1. Coat the inside of your saggar or biscuited stoneware bowl with silica about 1/8″ deep. To do this, mix the silica with water until it is the consistency of a medium-thick slip. Next, brush the silica slip onto the inside of the saggar, onto the bottom, and about 1/2″ above the maximum depth of your frit mixture. A frit boils when it is fired. Permit the silica-coated saggar or bowl to dry thoroughly before you fire it. A day or two of drying should be sufficient.

2. While your saggar is drying, weigh out all the materials required for the frit. Mix them thoroughly and screen them twice through a 60-mesh screen. You should mix about 2000 grams of material to fire at one time. You may want to divide the mixture among several bowls for fritting, since the thinner your frit cake is, the easier it will be to crush. After the materials are thoroughly mixed together, spread them in the saggars or bowls without disturbing the silica lining. About a 1″ thickness of mixed materials is probably best.

3. Fire the frit mixtures just to their melting temperature; do not overfire them or the frit may take the silica lining of the saggar or bowl into solution with it. Each frit has its own specific melting temperature and you should check out a small amount of each one first to find its melting point. Then proceed to fire the large batch.

4. After firing, you will have a cake of glass, which will probably be opaque and full of bubbles. When you take the glass cake from the saggar, scrape all the silica from the underside of the cake. Scrubbing with a stiff bristle or wire brush will help remove the silica. When free of silica, crush the glass (the frit) in the iron mortar until it looks like granulated sugar, then grind it on the ball mill for about 72 hours. If you have no ball mill, you may grind the frit in the iron mortar until it becomes fine enough. When ground, the frit should pass through a 200-mesh lawn.

Preparing Fritted Glazes

A completely fritted glaze is very much like fine sand, and it will settle to the bottom of the spray-gun jar when mixed with water. You should prepare your fritted glazes by mixing them with just enough water to pass them through a 60-mesh screen. Use a rubber kidney to work them through. Then add a thick gum tragacanth solution until the glaze can be sprayed.

You will learn the correct thickness for your glazes only from experience. However, remember that crystal frits should be applied more thinly than other glaze compositions — about 1/32″ is usually adequate. The reason for this is that crystal frits melt suddenly and become quite fluid. If too heavily applied, the frits tend to flow too freely, and you may find all the crystals on the brick slab beneath the pieces or on the kiln shelf.

When you have sprayed a very thin coat of glaze on the piece, let the piece dry and then fire it according to the schedule described for commercial frit glazes.

Crystal-Frit Compositions

As I mentioned earlier, crystal frits may be used alone or in combination with others. You will find suggestions about their uses along with the compositions of the individual frits which follow. I present frit compositions here because I have received letters after every exhibition in which my work has appeared requesting information on my crystalline glazes. For those who are interested, the following are the compositions of the frits I use in my glazes.

Frit -S- #1 (cone 9 – 12)

Powdered sodium carbonate	212 pbw
Powdered potassium carbonate	404
Zinc oxide (St. Joe #17)	486
Silica (250-mesh)	900
Titanium oxide	400

Note: This frit is designed to be used with other frits. Combinations of this and frit #15 may be sensational. St. Joe #17 zinc oxide is partially calcined and works well in frits.

Frit -S- #12 (cone 10 – 12)

Powdered potassium carbonate	414 pbw
Zinc oxide (St. Joe #17)	567
Silica	1200

Note: Excellent alone or in combination with other frits.

Frit -S- #3 (cone 10 – 12)

Powdered sodium carbonate	424 pbw

| Zinc oxide (St. Joe #17) | 486 |
| Silica | 1200 |

Note: Excellent alone or in combination with other frits.

Frit -S- #4a (cone 10 – 12)

Magnesium carbonate	84 pbw
Powdered sodium carbonate	318
Zinc oxide (St. Joe #17)	486
Silica	1200

Note: Excellent alone or in combination with other frits.

Frit -S- #4b (cone 10 – 12)

Calcined "K" grade magnesium	60.45 pbw
Powdered sodium carbonate	265.00
Zinc oxide (St. Joe #17)	486.00
Silica	1200.00

Note: Alone, this frit is a matte with circular white dots. Excellent when combined with frits 2, 3, 15, 16a. Do not combine with 4a.

Frit #15 (cone 10 – 12)

Powdered potassium carbonate	552 pbw
Zinc oxide (St. Joe #17)	648
Silica	1200

Note: An old but excellent frit. Works very well alone and in combination with others.

Frit #16a (cone 10 – 12)

Powdered potassium carbonate	276 pbw
Zinc oxide (St. Joe #17)	808
Silica	1200

Note: With copper, this frit is a turquoise matte at cone 12. An excellent frit to combine with others.

Frit #LM (cone 10 –12)

Lithium carbonate	296 pbw
Zinc oxide (St. Joe #17)	486
Silica	1200

Note: Use this one in small amounts (5% to 20%) in combination with others. A very interesting glaze when used alone with copper but may shiver from porcelain or cause the piece to dunt (shatter).

Frit Combinations

The following frit combinations produce excellent crystalline glazes. They should be fired at cone 10 down, cone 11 touching, held for three hours at 2080°F. (1140°C.).

Glaze #1

| Frit #1 | 30% |
| Frit #15 | 70% |

Glaze #2

Frit #1	25%
Frit #2	50%
Frit #3	25%

Glaze #3

| Frit #2 | 50% |
| Frit #3 | 50% |

Glaze #4

| Frit #1 | 40% |
| Frit #3 | 60% |

Glaze A7

Frit #1	20%
Frit #15	80%
Red iron oxide	6% by addition

Note: Huge brown-gold crystals on orange ground.

Glaze OR

Frit LM	30%
Frit #15	70%
Manganese oxide	2% by addition
Cobalt oxide	2.5% by addition

Note: Huge blue crystals on gray-blue ground.

Glaze F 62 – 19

Frit LM	50%
S #3	50%
Manganese oxide	2% by addition

Note: Excellent pale lavender crystals on pale tan transparent ground.

Glaze Z – F 62

| Frit #15 | 75.00 pbw |
| Frit #1 | 10.00 |

Frit #LM	40.00
Frit #16a	25.00
Manganese oxide	2.00
Molybdic oxide	.25
Copper oxide	1.00

Note: A good gray, large crystals.

Glaze OL

Frit #3	80 pbw
Frit S #1	20
Nickel oxide	2

Note: Blue-green on chartreuse background.

Complex Crystal-frit Glazes

If you want to get more mileage out of your crystal frits, use them in more complex glazes, such as the following. The advantage, if there is one, to these glazes is that you get a much larger quantity of glaze using less frit. In planning complex glazes, use a minimum of alumina or clay, as well as boron, since, in most instances, these substances tend to retard crystal formation.

Crystal-frit Glaze (cone 10 – 11)

Eureka feldspar	35.00 pbw
Silica	25.00
Whiting	20.00
Zinc oxide	35.00
Rutile	5.00
Frit #1	35.00

Crystal-frit Glaze (cone 11)

Kona F4 feldspar	40.00 pbw
Silica	30.00
Whiting	20.00
English china clay	7.50
Zinc oxide	40.00
Frit #15	40.00
Frit #16a	20.00
Rutile	7.50

Color in Fritted Zinc Silicate Glazes

In developing a glaze, it is customary to first calculate the basic glaze and then to calculate the percent of each material present. The percentage of coloring oxide is then expressed *in addition* to 100% of the glaze base. In order to find the percentage of each material in a glaze described in parts by weight, divide the parts by weight of each material by the total parts by weight of all materials present in the glaze.

Occasionally, as in the copper red glazes, the coloring material as well as the reducing material are parts of the total percentage of the glaze. This occurs in glazes that have been developed through triaxial blends — that is, three complete glazes, including colorants and reducing agents, that have been blended to create a new glaze.

The colors that develop in crystalline glazes are frequently a surprise, usually a pleasant one. They seem to have a definite influence on the patterns, as well as the shapes, of the crystals formed. It is not possible to predict what colors you will get, because they vary with different combinations of frits. However, the following is a list of the most often used coloring oxides and some of the colors that result from them. The percentages of the oxides listed here are only for crystalline glazes fired in an oxidizing fire.

Cobalt oxide. Almost always blue on a lighter blue ground, although blue-green on a cream ground has occurred. Use in quantities of .5% to 3%.

Copper oxide. A great variety of shades of green on a green ground. May also result in gray-green with black in the background, or green on cream, and a fine turquoise blue is not uncommon. Silver also develops on turquoise. Use 1% to 3%.

Nickel oxide. Produces silver stars on brown, strong blue on amber, blue-green on chartreuse. Use 1% to 3%.

Manganese oxide (MnO_2). Results in pale lavender-pink on tan ground; also orange, tan, and strong brown colors, as well as light purple. Use 1% to 4%.

Iron oxide. Produces gold on brown, brown-gold on orange, large brown-gold crystals with pink centers on a speckled tan ground, and golden brown on a maroon background. Use 2% to 6%.

Uranium. Yellow to gold on a yellow ground. Sodium uranate is best. Use 6% to 12%.

Tungsten. Produces highly lustrous surfaces, especially in combination with other oxides. Use 1% to 2%.

Many of the oxides listed work well in combination with others. Use two or three in a glaze and the result will surprise you.

Preparing Crystalline-Glazed Pieces

Expect crystalline glazes to be fluid and to flow down the side of the piece. In fact, you may quite

often find it necessary to grind a glaze from the foot of the piece. To reduce the amount of grinding required, try making pedestals for your pieces. Use porous insulating brick cut with a saw and filed or ground to the exact size of the base of the piece. If you are firing to cone 10, use #2400 porous brick for the pedestal and base. For pieces to be fired to cone 12, use #2600 brick.

Coat the pedestal with two or three coatings of kiln wash composed of 50% china clay or kaolin and 50% silica mixed with water to a creamlike consistency. Cut another 1/2″ slab from the flat surface of the brick, then cut that into two pieces about 4″ x 4 1/2″. Wash one slab with kiln wash as you did the pedestal, and permit both the slab and pedestal to dry.

Only crystalline-glazed pieces should be stacked in the kiln at one firing. When you are ready to fire, place the washed slab on the kiln floor or shelf, then place the pedestal on the center of the slab. Finally, place the piece so that the foot lines up exactly with the edges of the pedestal. Excess fluid glaze will run down the side of the piece onto the pedestal. If it runs beyond the pedestal, it will be caught by the slab underneath, saving kiln shelves from being damaged. After firing, you can easily grind the pedestals away without chipping the foot of the piece.

Lining Crystalline-Glazed Pieces

The following is a good transparent glaze for lining crystalline glazed pots.

Lining Glaze

Kona F4 feldspar	27 pbw
Whiting	20
China clay	20
Silica	33

Note: This glaze is transparent and has worked well from cone 9 to cone 12. Very narrow-necked porcelain pieces can be glazed without a lining glaze with no undesirable effects.

Firing Crystalline-Glazed Pieces

Since a reducing atmosphere inhibits crystal formation, avoid using reducing conditions when firing crystalline glazes. Leave the kiln door slightly open until the gum tragacanth has burned out of the glaze completely. Then you can seal the door with coils or wads of scrap clay. Apparently the gum tragacanth burning out of the piece produces enough carbon in the kiln to upset the chemical balance that permits crystal formation in the glaze.

Crystalline-glazed pieces may be re-fired, although the crystal pattern will change. It is about a fifty-fifty proposition — the piece may be greatly improved or it may not. For re-firing, it is usually desirable to add a thin film of glaze before stacking the ware. This may be the original glaze or another crystalline glaze.

This crystalline-glazed piece is shown mounted on a pedestal and a kiln-washed porous brick slab after firing.

The star-like shapes produced by the molybdenum crystal show up dramatically under the shortwave black light.

OTHER TYPES OF CRYSTALLINE GLAZES

In addition to zinc orthosilicate crystals, there are a number of other types of crystals that develop in glazes. The most common types are molybdenum, chromium, aventurine, and titanium crystals. In this chapter I will discuss each of these types separately and recommend the firing and holding temperatures, as well as procedures, to use with each.

Molybdenum Crystals

The molybdenum crystal is usually not very large and is most often a distorted rectangle, diamond, or star in shape. Much work has been done to date with zinc silicate crystals, but very little has been done with molybdenum crystals; the following are some probable reasons for this.

Molybdenum is more commonly used as an opacifier in enamels for metal and as a coloring agent in glass and glazes.

Molybdenum crystals are somewhat elusive and less predictable than zinc silicate crystals.

Molybdenum crystals are subtle and lack the strong contrast of form and pattern found in zinc crystals.

Physical Properties of Molybdic Oxide

Consideration of some of the physical properties of molybdic (molybdenum) oxide may provide us with a key to its performance in glazes. First, we should consider the behavior of molybdic oxide (MoO_3) at elevated temperatures.

Sublimation begins at 1292°F. (700°C.). This means that molybdic oxide starts to pass from a solid to a gaseous state at that temperature. Actually, it passes from a solid to a gaseous state and condenses to a solid form again without liquifying, and we can therefore safely say that some of it must be lost as it vaporizes.

Molybdic oxide melts at 1463°F. (795°C.) and boils at 2111°F. (1155°C.). It therefore boils before cone 9, which deforms at 2336°F. (1280°C.) when fired at an increase of 302°F. (150°C.) per hour. Traces of basic oxide material reduce the vapor pressure of molybdic oxide, which may explain why molybdic oxide remains in a glaze even when raised above its boiling point.

Both yellow and bluish colors result when molybdenum is fired at as high as cone 12.

Next, we should consider the crystal structure of molybdic oxide. Molybdic oxide forms rhombic tablets (six sided prisms whose faces are parallelograms). From the molten state molybdic oxide undergoes considerable expansion on solidifying, and forms rhombic, needle-like crystals. The rhombic crystals formed have a layered structure that is rare among oxides. Each layer consists of parallel rows of distorted octahedra which are MoO_6. The six oxygen atoms occupy the corners and the Mo atom the center of each octahedron. The octahedra within each layer are joined by the edges and corners.

The crystals are highly dispersing and strongly double refracting. In other words they separate complex light into its different colored rays which are deflected from a straight path at two points. This results in a most interesting quality in a molybdic oxide crystal, which is the concentration of spectral colors at its center. Moreover, the needles are so thin that they appear as layers of thin colored film in the glaze.

We should also keep in mind the potential of molybdic oxide to be reduced to a lower form of the oxide. This reduction is brought about superficially by the action of light and atmospheric dust and is what causes the faint bluish or greenish cast sometimes seen in the oxide.

Molybdic oxide is outstanding when used to reduce surface tension — as a wetting agent — in the melt of the glaze.

When used in small amounts, molybdenum promotes the formation of other types of crystals in the glaze. Glazes containing molybdenum may opalesce when they are reheated.

It is also interesting that molybdenum crystals will form in a glaze with a relatively high lead content, although lead is not necessary for their development.

When you work with molybdenum crystals, do not hesitate to re-fire pieces on which no crystals have developed. Crystals may appear on re-firing with or without the application of additional glaze.

Fuming Property of Molybdenum

Another very interesting feature of molybdenum is its fuming ability: when fired near a glaze containing molybdenum, certain glazes which contain no molybdenum will sometimes develop crystals. This unusual phenomenon opens the door for much experimentation. What actually happens is that the molybdenum vaporizes at 1292°F. (700°C.), settles in either a vaporous or solidified form on the surface of a glaze that will permit molybdenum crystals to form, and proceeds to crystallize. However, it has not been determined how extensively this can be made to occur, or which glaze composition is best for fuming crystals from molybdenum.

Molybdenum Crystal Glaze Compositions

Although much more work needs to be done with molybdenum crystal glazes, the following suggestions may offer you a starting point for achieving exciting results. These glazes are very sensitive, and the results are not as yet consistently predictable. Don't give up on the first few tries, however. Continue experimenting even to the point of repeating an experiment under a variety of firing conditions.

Try using straight line blends or triaxial blends to combine the various recipes.

Firing seems to produce better results when several pots coated with the same glaze are placed close to one another in the kiln.

Try re-firing with and without additional glaze applications.

Try variations in firing schedules and firing temperatures for these compositions.

Explore the use of various coloring oxides in these glazes.

Comments following the various molybdenum crystal glaze compositions describe the results that have been obtained under certain firing conditions, although it cannot be predicted that these results will occur consistently.

L.H. #4 (cone 4)

Litharge	39.48 pbw
Lithium carbonate	4.37
Whiting	5.30
Strontium	4.37
Edgar plastic kaolin	22.85
Silica	23.02
Molybdic oxide	4% by addition

Note: When fired in an oxidizing atmosphere in a closely stacked Globar kiln with normal heating and cooling, the glaze has become quite fluid, collecting in transparent pools in the bottoms of bowls. Large 1″ crystals occurred in the glaze.

SN Glaze (cone 3)

White lead	43.67 pbw
Barium carbonate	3.33
Zinc oxide	4.11
Strontium carbonate	2.51
Dolomite	3.11
Colemanite (gerstley borate)	3.00
Whiting	3.96
Edgar plastic kaolin	10.92
Silica	25.30
Molybdic oxide	4% by addition
Titanium oxide	4% by addition

Note: When fired to cone 3 in an oxidizing atmosphere in a Globar electric kiln, this has become a glossy glaze with many star-shaped, iridescent crystals up to 1/2″ in diameter.

R.P.S. Glaze (cone 3)

White lead	47.40 pbw
Whiting	7.36
Zinc oxide	8.94
Edgar plastic kaolin	10.92
Silica	22.03
Molybdic oxide	4% by addition
Titanium oxide	4% by addition

Note: When fired to cone 3 in a Globar electric kiln, this glaze formed a yellow-tan matte with many star-shaped iridescent crystals 1/2″ in diameter, collected in a pool at the bottom of the bowl. The outside of the piece was an iridescent matte.

MA #1 Glaze (cone 9)

Kingman feldspar	39.489 pbw
Whiting	7.199
Barium carbonate	1.864
Zinc oxide	7.091
Colemanite	16.666
Silica	22.201
Molybdic oxide	4% by addition
Titanium oxide	8% by addition

Note: When fired to cone 9 in a Globar electric kiln, this and the following three glazes have displayed a milky blue background with star-shaped and rectangular crystals with iridescent centers.

MA #2 Glaze (cone 9)

Pemco frit #P 54	37.882 pbw
Barium carbonate	1.927
Whiting	2.537
Bone ash	.687
China clay	31.888
Silica	17.526
Molybdic oxide	6% by addition
Titanium oxide	4% by addition

MA #3 Glaze (cone 9)

Pemco frit #P 239	40.522 pbw
Barium carbonate	1.943
Kingman feldspar	3.435
Zinc oxide	7.459
China clay	20.195

Whiting	9.932
Molybdic oxide	4% by addition
Rutile	6% by addition

MA #4 Glaze (cone 9)

O. Hommel frit #5	22.034 pbw
Zinc oxide	7.171
Barium carbonate	1.869
Colemanite	7.698
Whiting	11.446
China clay	24.473
Silica	25.308
Molybdic oxide	4% by addition
Titanium oxide	6% by addition

Chromium Crystal Glaze Compositions

It is well known that chromium produces crystals at quite low temperatures. These are the basic requirements for producing red crystalline glazes from the following compositions.

Silica should not exceed 10% of the composition of the batch.

A lead glaze is essential. Red lead oxide seems superior to litharge or white lead. The lead content of the glaze should be approximately 75% to 80%.

The alumina content should be low. When introduced as clay, it should not exceed 10% of the batch.

Soda ash and calcium tend to promote a matte finish, rather than a crystal pattern.

Zinc oxide, if used, should not exceed 1% of the batch; a greater quantity seems to work against the development of a crystal pattern.

Barium carbonate may be used for up to 4% of the batch.

The glaze should not be fired above cone 09 (1760°F.). Above this temperature, the color changes from red to green, and the crystals are lost.

A half hour of grinding on the ball mill improves the probability of crystal formation.

Firing between cone 014 and 010 seems to produce the best crystals.

Biscuit should be fired to complete maturity for the ware before the glaze is applied.

Firing time should be from room temperature to cone 013 in three hours.

The glaze should be applied in a thin coating.

Chromium Crystal Glaze #1

Red lead	80 pbw
Silica	8
Kaolin	5
Chromium oxide	7

Chromium Crystal Glaze #2

Red lead	81.87 pbw
Silica	5.42
Kona F4 feldspar	11.05
Barium carbonate	3.91
Chromium oxide	5.06

Red Crystalline Matte

Red lead	75 pbw
China clay	10
Whiting	4
Zinc oxide	1
Soda ash	5
Silica	7
Chromium oxide	8

Note: Fired in a small Amaco kiln.

CCI – Chromium Crystals (cone 012 – 010)

Red lead	80 pbw
Flint	10
Potash feldspar	10
Chromium oxide	6

Note: This gives large, plumelike crystals of brilliant red color.

Chromium Crystals (cone 010)

Red lead	75 pbw
Georgia China clay	10
Flint	7
Chromium	8
Whiting	4
Zinc oxide	1
Soda ash	5

Aventurine Crystals

Aventurine crystals are small platelike particles suspended in a transparent glaze. Light strikes them to produce a glistening gold-stone effect. These crystals may be produced by saturating the glaze with iron — or another metallic oxide such as chromium or uranium — which dissolves in the glass magma during the firing process. As the glaze is then slowly cooled, the excess iron produces crystals. The quantity of iron required to produce crystals varies, depending on the basic composition of the glaze and the quantity of iron that will dissolve in the glaze. Some glazes may contain as little as 5%, while others may require 20% iron in order to produce satisfactory crystal formations. Over-saturation produces a brownish, crystalline matte or scum on the surface of the glaze.

Aventurine Crystal Glaze Compositions

The basic composition of the aventurine glaze varies widely, but glazes containing a high percentage of lead and soda (sodium oxide) seem to produce the best results. The alumina, silica, and boron content should be consistent with the maturing temperature of the glaze. Using calcium as a basic oxide is neither detrimental nor particularly beneficial to the formation of crystals.

The nature of the crystals produced depends on the basic composition of the glaze, the amount of crystallizing element used, the firing process, and particularly upon the cooling period — slow and prolonged cooling is necessary for satisfactory results. However, a holding period such as that used for zinc silicate crystals does not seem necessary.

The following suggested compositions for aventurine glazes make use of frits that are commercially available. Commercial frits are desirable in aventurine glazes because they contain high percentages of lead and sodium which are conducive to crystal formation.

RM #1 Aventurine Glaze (cone 06 and cone 4)

O. Hommel frit #71	100 pbw
Bentonite	3
Red iron oxide	8

Note: When applied to a red clay and to Jordan clay, this mixture produced a dark, red-brown glaze with aventurine crystals at cone 06, and a maroon, almost black glaze with aventurine crystals at cone 4. The addition of small percentages of zinc did not detract from the quality of the crystals produced. The addition of 10% feldspar resulted in a red-brown glaze without crystals that crazed on both clays at cone 06; the color was a more definite red on the Jordan clay. At cone 4, the addition of feldspar produced a dull brownish black without crystals.

RL #7 Aventurine Glaze (cone 06)

Ferro frit #5301	100 pbw

Bentonite	3
Red iron oxide	20

Note: When fired to cone 06 on stoneware clay previously biscuited to cone 9, this mixture crazed badly but produced a brown, transparent glaze with many pinpoint, gold-colored crystals.

RL #V7 Aventurine Glaze (cone 06)

O. Hommel frit #25	100 pbw
Bentonite	3
Red iron oxide	15

Note: When fired to cone 06 on stoneware clay previously biscuited to cone 9, this mixture crazed badly but produced a golden brown, transparent glaze with many very small, gold-colored crystals.

RL #V9 Aventurine Glaze (cone 06)

O. Hommel frit #33	100.00 pbw
Bentonite	3.00
Red iron oxide	20.00
Black copper oxide	.50

Note: This mixture has produced a dark brown, semi-gloss glaze with many small gold and red crystals. The crystals were most brilliant on a red clay body biscuited to cone 4.

Fluidity of Aventurine Glazes

The frits listed in the above compositions are conducive to the development of aventurine crystals when iron is used as a colorant. They may be used for the development of aventurine glazes at a variety of temperatures, as long as measures are taken to adjust the fluidity of the glaze at each temperature. This adjustment may be accomplished through the addition of the following oxides:

The addition of boron (B_2O_3) reduces fluidity. However, this should not be used in excessive amounts or it may retard crystal formation.

The addition of silica (SiO_2) reduces fluidity and is not detrimental to crystalline development.

Titanium Crystals

Titanium oxide (TiO_2) and rutile (titanium oxide with an iron contamination) are well known as materials that crystallize in glazes. My experience with titanium crystals indicates that, in general, they are not as spectacular or as interesting as zinc orthosilicate crystals. As a result, not nearly so much time has been devoted to studying them.

When added to almost any glaze, both titanium

oxide and rutile act as matting agents — that is, they change the surface of the glaze from glossy to matte. The reason for this is that the titanium turns into microscopic, needlelike crystals; these are present in such great quantities that when the light strikes the surface of the glaze, it is broken up by the crystals and reflected out in all directions, causing the surface of the glaze to appear non-reflective or matte. Usually 8% to 10% of titanium is sufficient to produce a silky kind of matte surface. Greater quantities produce so many crystals that the surface becomes rough to the touch.

When fired at low temperatures — cone 06 to cone 04 — many lead glazes to which titanium has been added will develop titanium crystals about 1/8″ in diameter. Although these crystals are un-interesting in themselves, they very often form in "ropes" down the side of a piece; in contrast to glossy background, these ropes of crystals may give low-fire pieces an interesting textural quality. Again, between 8% and 10% of titanium is sufficient to cause these crystals to form. When coloring agents are added to such glazes, the crystals are usually a somewhat darker version of the glossy background.

You will frequently find titanium in a zinc orthosilicate crystal glaze. The reason for this is that titanium acts to promote crystal growth from other crystallizing agents. When used for this purpose, titanium should usually not exceed a 5% addition to the batch; quite frequently, 3% is adequate. Try this procedure in a crystal glaze that has not been working satisfactorily — the titanium addition should aid in the production of crystals.

Firing Procedure. The titanium crystal glaze compositions listed here should be fired to cone 9. In an Alpine Globar kiln, the schedule follows:

1. Set all switches on low or Step 1 for 1 hour.

2. Set all switches on medium or Step 2 for 1 hour.

3. Set all switches on high or Step 3 (cone 9 down) for 4½ hours.

4. Cool to 2021°F. (1100°C.) and hold at that temperature for 3 hours on medium or Step 2.

Titanium Crystal Glaze Compositions

VI-D Titanium Crystal Glaze (cone 9)

Ferro frit #3134	20%
Pemco frit #P 283	50%
Titanium oxide	10%
Silica	20%

Note: The resulting glaze is a white gloss covered with gold, needle-shaped crystals 1/4″ to 1/2″ long.

XII Titanium Crystal Glaze (cone 9)

O. Hommel K3 frit	50.78%	60%	65%
Titanium oxide	10.00%	10%	10%
Silica	39.32%	30%	25%

Note: Three variations of this glaze are listed. All three work well, but the third seems to produce the best results.

I-B Titanium Crystal Glaze (cone 8–10)

O. Hommel K3 frit	70%
Titanium oxide	10%
Silica	20%

Note: This glaze is closely related to the three combinations above, but was fired at three different cones — 8, 9, and 10. The result was fair at cone 8, good at cone 9, and crystals were few and scattered at cone 10.

Temmoku Crystal Glazes

The ancient Chinese temmoku glazes are considered by some to have been the first glazes to contain crystals. These glazes were first used on the tea bowls of the Zen monks who had a monastery on the mountain Tien Mu Shan; temmoku, sometimes spelled tenmoku, was named after this mountain. There is currently a wide variety of temmoku glazes in use, many of which have been given such romantic names as "oil spot," "hare's fur," "alligator skin," "lizard skin," and "partridge feather," as well as "kaki," which is rust red in color.

I include the temmoku glazes with other types of crystalline glazes because I believe they are aventurine in origin; although I do not know the specific relationship between temmoku glazes and the iron red glazes, there are definite similarities between these two types of specialized glazes. For example, all the color variations found in the temmoku glazes are the result of iron contained in the composition; rock or clay similar in iron composition to the Albany clay slip used on current temmoku ware was probably the basis of the early temmoku glazes. Also, the contemporary Japanese oil spot temmoku glazes contain many aventurine crystals in the background matrix, and the oil spots themselves may be concentrations of aventurine crystals.

Preparing Oil Spot Glazes

Since the basic composition of the oil spot temmoku glaze — which is based primarily on a clay slip — can be varied to create glazes that resemble the hare's fur, alligator and lizard skin, and kaki

*This oil spot bowl was made
by Morikazu Kimura,
a contemporary Japanese potter.*

varieties, we should begin by discussing how to prepare and use this composition. Like all the color variations in temmoku glazes, oil spots are concentrations of iron in metallic crystalline or oxidized form, depending on the materials used in combination with the Albany slip. The domestic clays that contain iron and therefore most closely resemble temmoku ware when used as glazes are Albany and Michigan slip clays. Albany slip in particular contains enough iron to produce a full black or brown-black glaze at cone 9.

However, although it is a completely vitrified brown-black glass, the Albany slip is non-fluid at cone 9. It is therefore necessary to increase the fluidity of the glaze in which Albany slip is used in order to provide an opportunity for the desired oil spot pattern to develop. The glaze can be made more fluid by the introduction of feldspar and borax as fluxing agents. A limited amount of kaolin or ball clay should then be added to prevent over-fluidity while the glaze is molten, and iron oxide should also be added to stimulate the concentration of iron that produces the crystalline oil spot pattern.

Applying Oil Spot Glazes

It has been my experience that the slip should be applied to a coarse-grained clay body when the piece is in the late stages of leather-hardness, and that some time should elapse between the applications to the inside and outside of the piece. Otherwise, the coarse-grained quality of the clay may cause the piece to slump when it is saturated with the water contained in the slip. When you use a fine-grained clay such as Jordan, you may glaze both the inside and outside during the medium leather-hard stage, without a drying period between applications. I have found that slip-glazing dry ware results in cracking of the pot, and applying calcined Albany slip clay to the biscuit has no appeal for me.

Basic Oil Spot Glaze Composition

Contrary to some potters' insistence that a reduction fire is necessary for oil spot development, I have found that oil spot glazes of a superior quality can be produced at between cone 9 and 10 in an oxidizing fire. Glazes containing materials that result in oil spot development at cone 9 pass through a bubbling process before the spots form; the spots are the direct result of the bubbles, and each spot marks the area where a bubble occurred.

As you work with the following glaze compositions, remember that the firing is extremely important in the production of oil spots; over-firing will cause them to disappear completely. Do not use a prolonged cooling period such as the holding period you would use for zinc silicate crystals, as it is not only unnecessary but may be detrimental to the results. The following oil spot glaze composition and variations produce most satisfactory results when applied to leather-hard clay pieces.

FM Oil Spot Temmoku (cone 9)

Albany slip	46.50 pbw
Kona F4 spar	37.20
Kentucky ball clay	9.30
Red iron oxide	4.70
Borax	2.30

Note: When fired, this glaze has a black background and circular oil spots that display a silvery sheen in reflected, or indirect, light; when placed in direct sunlight, the spots are red-brown in color. In order to produce a satisfactory oil spot pattern, the glaze should be applied rather heavily. Jordan clay provides a suitable body for the ware.

Variations in the Oil Spot Glaze Composition

The variations obtainable from Albany slip with additions of other materials are unlimited. Other temmoku type glazes displaying aventurine crystals can be made by combining Albany slip with a 20% addition of burnt umber, Albany slip with a 20% addition of red iron oxide, and Albany slip with a 20% addition of black iron oxide, and firing at cone 12 to 13. The following are more interesting variations that can be made from Albany slip, which is the basis of the oil spot glaze composition.

Oil Spot Glaze Variation

Albany slip	100.00
Rutile	10.00
Apricot ash	12.50

Note: When fired to cone 9, this combination results in a brown and gold mottled, feathery, crystalline matte; when fired to cone 11, it has a brownish color with overlapping gold crystals.
A similar crystal glaze, which is lighter in color, results when Albany slip with a 25% addition of magnesium carbonate is fired at cone 11 to 13. At the same temperature, a 25% addition of fluorspar to Albany slip results in a fluid, noncrystalline, transparent, crazed, brownish green glaze.

Oil Spot Glaze Variation (cone 8 – 9)

Albany slip	100 pbw
Yellow ochre	10
Lepidolite	5

Note: This combination results in a brownish black glaze with large red-brown oil spots.

Oil Spot Glaze Variation (cone 8 – 9)

Albany slip	100 pbw
Burnt umber	10

Note: This combination results in a black glaze with small silver oil spots.

Oil Spot Glaze Variation (cone 8 – 9)

Albany slip	100 pbw
Burnt sienna	10
Lepidolite	5

Note: This combination results in a dark brown glaze with large red oil spots.

Oil Spot Glaze Variation (cone 8 – 9)

Albany slip	100.00
Red iron oxide	10.00
Buckingham feldspar	5.00
Rutile	10.00

Note: This combination results in a red-brown glaze with silver-red oil spots.

Oil Spot Glaze Variation (cone 8 – 9)

Albany slip	100.00 pbw
Eureka feldspar	5.00
Rutile	10.00

Note: This combination results in a chestnut brown glaze with circular, mustard yellow spots.

Other Temmoku Glaze Compositions

The hare's fur glaze can be made from a mixture similar to those used for the oil spot glazes, provided the composition is made fluid enough to cause the iron concentrations to become streaks rather than spots, as well as to cause a roll of glaze to form above the foot rim of the piece. When fired to cone 9 on Jordan clay, Albany slip with an addition of 5% rutile produces a dark brown glaze with a light brown spotted texture. This light brown color somewhat resembles the hare's fur markings of the Chinese hare's fur temmoku, although this glaze is not fluid enough to develop the true streaked pattern of the Sung pieces that date from around 1000 A.D. However, if it is sufficiently fluxed, a composition of Albany slip and 5% to 10% rutile may produce the true hare's fur markings of these temmoku wares.

When the following composition is fired at cone 10 to 11, the result is a black glaze with aventurine crystals dispersed throughout and red-brown mottling that somewhat resembles hare's fur in areas where the glaze was fluid.

Temmoku Glaze

Albany slip	50 pbw
Plastic Vitrox	25
Kentucky ball clay #4	5
Powdered borax	10
Apricot ash	10
Black iron oxide	10

Alligator and lizard skin effects can be produced by applying Albany slip alone to biscuited Jordan clay and gloss firing the pieces to cone 4. The kaki glaze develops when the FM oil spot glaze listed earlier is fired to cone 12 or 13.

COPPER REDUCTION GLAZES

There are many conditions, or variables, that can effect the results of reduction firing. These include the composition of the particular glaze used; the atmospheric conditions inside and outside the kiln, such as gas pressure, wind velocity, and wind direction; and your manipulation of the kiln during the firing process. Although kiln procedures were briefly discussed in an earlier chapter, if you wish to fire your own pieces, you will need to know more about the actual reactions involved in reduction firing so that you can use the procedures effectively to create the desired results.

Regardless of efforts to duplicate a particular set of firing conditions exactly, no two firings are ever identical. Although the results of similar firings should be similar, you will find some more interesting than others. It is largely this elusive nature of the results that makes working with copper reduction glazes so interesting.

Reduction Firing

As described earlier, reduction firing is brought about during the firing process by decreasing the amount of oxygen in the atmosphere until that amount is insufficient to permit some of the oxides present in the glaze — and some of the oxides present in most stoneware bodies — to develop as they normally would under oxidizing conditions. When the amount of oxygen is reduced, excess carbon in the atmosphere seeks out and combines with oxygen atoms contained in some of the oxides present, thereby creating changes in color, and sometimes in texture. I say "some" of the oxides because not all the oxides used in glazes or bodies are affected by reduction. In fact, we could restrict ourselves exclusively to coloring oxides when discussing reduction if it were not for lead, which is also affected, and for the textural changes that sometimes occur. The cause of the textural changes is unknown, since, with the exception of lead, the basic acid, and neutral oxides normally used in glazes are so stable that reduction usually has very little, if any, effect on them.

Reduction of Copper

The normal, stable copper oxide molecule present in an oxidized glaze is cupric oxide (CuO), which consists of one atom of copper combined with one atom of oxygen. The carbon monoxide (CO) or pure carbon (C) present in a reducing atmosphere is greedy for oxygen; in order to form stable carbon dioxide molecules (CO_2), carbon atoms combine with oxygen from any source available. In this instance, the most readily available source is cupric

These three pieces were coated with Copper Reduction Glaze IV-4. The center piece was reduction fired and the others were oxidation fired.

oxide, which is the least stable oxide in the glaze.

The result is the formation of CO_2 molecules; this forces the CuO to become cuprous oxide (Cu_2O) and/or colloidal copper (Cu). Colloidal copper is metallic copper in the form of particles so small that their size is not comprehensible to us — it has been proposed that the probable diameter of such a particle is 4/100,000 of an inch. This is called a colloid because it is so finely divided. Unlike crystalloids, colloids are incapable of forming a true solution and cannot be crystallized. This change from CuO to Cu_2O or colloidal Cu is called reduction because the amount of oxygen in the cupric oxide molecule has been reduced by 50% to form the cuprous oxide molecule and by 100% to produce the colloidal copper particle.

Colors Obtained from Reduced Copper

When we reduce the cupric oxide molecule, an interesting thing takes place — it changes color. So that we can appreciate these changes, let us first discuss the colors that result when cupric oxide is fired in a normal oxidizing atmosphere. When dissolved in a lead glaze, cupric oxide, which is black, produces a green color under normal oxidizing firing conditions. In a highly alkaline glaze, particularly one rich in sodium, as well as in lithium glazes, cupric oxide produces a turquoise blue. In glazes containing the right amount of barium oxide, the color produced may be an intense Egyptian blue that is very difficult to describe. When subjected to reduction firing, the cupric oxide in an alkaline glaze of the right composition changes to cuprous oxide and/or colloidal copper, and brilliant red glaze colors result. These glazes are called copper reds. There are many degrees of reduction; therefore many variations of red result from different reduction firings. There are also other factors which influence the color of copper reduction glazes — for example, the proportion of the basic oxides, as well as that of the other materials, in the glaze. There is inconclusive evidence that increasing the calcium content of the glaze may result in a purple color. I have been told by other potters that a turquoise blue can be obtained from reduced copper if lithium and barium are present in the glaze, and I have seen copper reduction glazes in which an intense, almost cobalt blue has resulted. In my experience, I have found that almost unlimited variations in color are possible, including a slightly purple blue, gray and pink combinations, mottled purple with white flecks, purple with blue spots, red-violet with blue spots, variations of pink, pink and red, red with darker red spots, and so on, *ad infinitum*.

One of the most interesting features of copper reduction glazes is their unpredictability. The same glaze composition used in three or more separate firings may yield a different result each time. However, the result is always interesting and always has some sort of relationship to the original color. Another very interesting feature of these glazes is that a fired glaze that is disappointing in color may be sprayed with a different glaze and re-fired with almost invariably good results. Variations in color can also be created by spraying a light coat of a different glaze over a piece that has been glazed but not yet fired. If you try this double-spray glazing, apply your second glaze before the first glaze coat becomes too dry, or the glaze may crack and peel off before or during firing. If you have a sufficient supply of glaze and are skillful at dipping or pouring, you may use these procedures.

Reduction Firing by Kiln Adjustment

Now that you know what reduction firing is and how it effects copper, let us investigate how to achieve it. Reduction can be achieved by using one of two procedures or for some glazes, a combination of both. (Specific firing schedules for both procedures will be presented later on in this chapter.) The first procedure requires a fuel-burning kiln and involves manipulating the fuel supply, the dampers on the kiln, and the air supply to the firing chamber. Almost all reduction firing of this type starts out as oxidation firing — that is, initially there is sufficient air and therefore sufficient oxygen being drawn into the kiln to insure complete combustion, and the oxides within the glaze remain stable at this stage.

Oxidizing firing should be continued until the temperature in the kiln has reached at least 1200° to 1500°F. (650° to 820°C.) before reduction is begun. This is the lowest temperature range at which excess fuel can be broken down into its component parts — carbon monoxide and hydrogen — which will in turn be used to reduce the copper glazes. Excess fuel is the volume of fuel present in the kiln atmosphere in addition to that required for combustion with the volume of air present. Gas fuel is chiefly methane (CH_4) although it does contain some carbon monoxide and hydrogen, and most fuels contain hydrocarbons that are decomposed into hydrogen and carbon at the high temperature of combustion. The hydrogen burns immediately, while the free carbon must be heated until it is red hot or white hot before it will begin to burn. Perfect combustion, which can exist only in an oxygen-rich oxidizing atmosphere, produces a colorless flame.

This Alpine H.F.S. #2 kiln is set up for proper reduction firing.

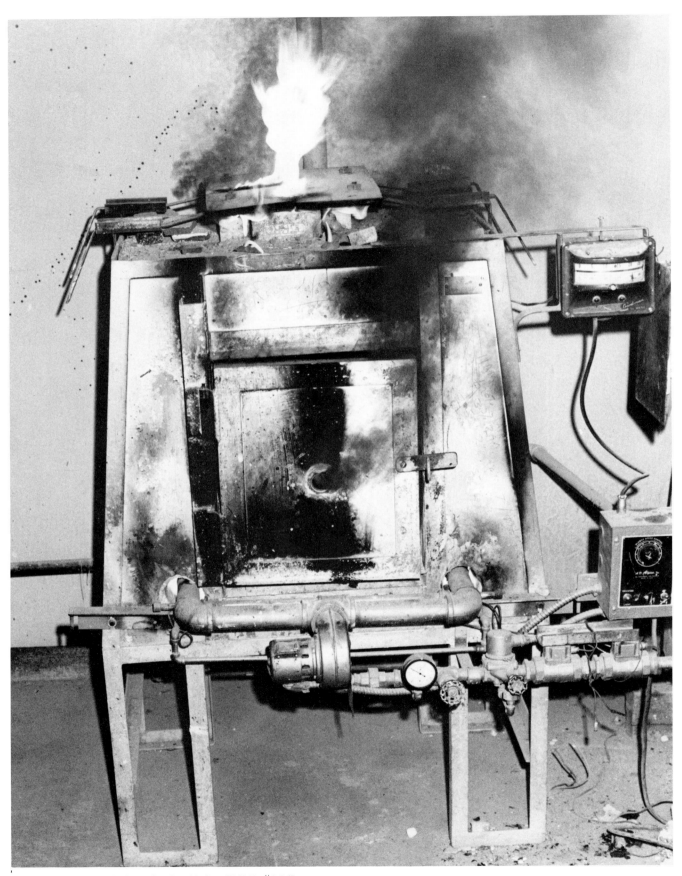

Poor reduction technique in the Alpine H.F.S. #2 kiln.

If you start reduction firing at between 1200° and 1500°F. (650° and 820°C.), you will get reduction of the body as well as the glaze. In order to achieve reducing conditions in the kiln at this temperature range, close down the dampers until all auxiliary draft ports are neutral — that is, until no air is being drawn into the kiln, around the burners, around the door, or at any additional draft ports your kiln may have. You should check these places with a lighted kitchen match; the flame should remain stationary, being neither drawn into the kiln nor blown out or away from the kiln. This neutral condition which lasts only a few minutes in the kiln is what the Japanese call a middle fire. Conditions should be balanced: you should have just enough oxygen for what we call neutral firing, there should be no excess oxygen and no excess carbon, and carbon dioxide should be present in the kiln atmosphere.

When you have achieved this neutral condition, in order to start reduction, you will probably need to increase the gas and possibly the air supply to insure a continued rise in temperature. When plugs are removed, the back pressure will cause a bluish green to purple haze, or light flame, to escape from the peep holes, and you should observe the same kind of haze at the damper of the kiln. When this occurs, it is considered to be ideal reduction firing. Ordinarily, such ideal reducing conditions are not achieved; there is a smokey atmosphere in the kiln, as well as some smoke and yellow flame at the damper. This is also a reducing condition, but not at its best.

Regardless of which condition exists, however, you will have an excess of carbon monoxide and doubtless some free carbon in the kiln chamber, and reduction will take place. The length of time you reduce and the exact temperature at which you start reduction will essentially be determined by how your glazes react, as well as by the type of result you wish to achieve. Keep in mind that in any kiln, over-reduction at an early stage of firing, before the glaze is melted, can cause the body to become impregnated with carbon. If heavy reduction is continued in the later stages of firing, this carbon may cause the ware to bloat. This seldom occurs when correct reduction procedure is followed. Remember also that in order for reduction to take place, it is not necessary to have clouds of smoke coming from your kiln.

Localized Reduction

The second procedure for the production of reduced glazes involves adding a reducing agent to the glaze itself. This is called localized reduction

because this procedure makes it possible to have reduced and oxidized areas on a single piece, as well as to fire one reduced piece in a kiln-load of ware in an oxidizing atmosphere.

Some years ago, Arthur Baggs and Edgar Littlefield conducted a study of copper glazes reduced in an oxidizing atmosphere, the report on which appeared in the *Journal of the American Ceramic Society* (see Bibliography). By using silicon carbide (SiC), better known as carborundum, as a reducing agent in copper glaze, they were able to produce copper reds. The same glaze fired without a reducing agent and with an increase in tin oxide produced a light blue color. This was used as a lining glaze for the red pieces, thus enabling them to use a copper red and a copper blue glaze on the same piece. They also used carborundum in a clay slip, which they applied under the blue glaze to produce a decorative red pattern surrounded by a blue glaze when fired. This combination looked much like the Chun red decoration on the blue-glazed pots of the Chinese Sung Dynasty.

The following is the empirical formula for the glaze used by Baggs and Littlefield.

$$\left.\begin{array}{l} .3\ Na_2O \\ .3\ K_2O \\ .4\ CaO \end{array}\right\} \quad \left.\begin{array}{l} .6\ Al_2O_3 \\ .4\ B_2O_3 \end{array}\right\} \quad \left\{ 4.\ SiO_2 \right.$$

To produce the red color, .3% copper carbonate, between .2% and 1% silicon carbide, and 1% tin oxide were added to the batch. The same empirical formula, with the addition of 7% tin oxide and .3% copper carbonate was used to produce the blue. The glazes were fired to cone 9 in a down-draft kiln under oxidizing firing conditions. The firing period was 24 hours; the kiln was then turned off and permitted to cool.

When silicon carbide is used as a reducing agent in a glaze, the heat of firing breaks it down into silicon and carbon. The equation is — SiC + heat = Si + C — which means that free silicon atoms and free carbon atoms are present in the glaze. Silicon cannot become a part of the glaze, as it must, until it has picked up oxygen and formed silica (SiO_2), the stable oxide of silicon found in any glaze. The carbon atom, as we have already discussed, is greedy for oxygen; it must therefore find and combine with oxygen in order to form carbon monoxide, or more likely carbon dioxide, which is its most stable molecule. The least stable oxide present is the cupric oxide, which either loses all its oxygen and becomes colloidal copper, or loses only part of its oxygen and forms cuprous oxide.

There are other raw materials in the glaze that contain excess oxygen and that dissociate under the action of heat. Some of these are feldspar, calcium carbonate, and raw borax. We could, then, set up the following theoretical equation, which is not a true chemical equation but which gives us a picture of the reducing action that probably takes place in the glaze: $CuO + Si + C + heat + un$known amounts of O from other materials $= Cu_2O + Cu + SiO_2 + CO_2$. Here we find copper reduced, silica in a form in which it can become part of the glaze, and carbon dioxide given off as gas.

Using Copper Carbonate

This is an appropriate place to explain why, when we have a choice, we usually prefer to use copper carbonate ($CuCO_3$) instead of cupric oxide. The reason is that because it contains a carbon atom, copper carbonate is even less stable than cupric oxide. When heated to high temperatures, copper carbonate decomposes. The equation for this reaction is — $CuCO_3 + heat = CuO + CO_2$. This decomposition leaves the oxide vulnerable to attack by the free carbon and free silicon in the glaze.

Other Reducing Agents and Procedures

For those who are interested in some original research on localized reduction, there are other reducing agents in addition to silicon carbide that can provide you with a field for study. For example, very little work has been done using powdered elemental silicon as a reducing agent, and still less has been done using powdered aluminum or aluminum carbide. As far as I know, nothing has been done using boron carbide as a reducing agent. Any of these agents should work, provided the right combinations of glaze and reducing agent can be found.

Continued work on the use of silicon carbide as a reducing agent has shown that its inclusion in glazes fired in a reducing atmosphere can also aid in reduction. The primary advantage of this procedure is a decrease in the length of time required for firing; this is brought about because the silicon carbide functions as a reducing agent within the glaze, while the reducing atmosphere hastens reduction from outside the glaze.

Bodies for Copper Reduction Glazes

Copper reduction glazes may be used on either stoneware or porcelain bodies but should not be used on coarse-grogged bodies. Although the reason is not known, coarse bodies often cause the glaze to blister; even when no blisters result, a coarse body may detract from the quality of the glaze.

In general, when you are relying on a glaze for the enhancement of the form, the body of the ware should contribute to and not detract from the overall effect. When you are relying on the body to provide textural quality or interest, glazes should be used quite sparingly — or only for contrast. We should therefore keep in mind that the more unusual glazes have unique qualities that should be used to the greatest advantage. Sometimes a simple form, uncomplicated by throwing ridges, will provide the proper background for such glazes; at other times, the ridges may be more desirable, depending on the glaze and on the overall effect desired.

Most copper reduction glazes display the color of the body on the lips, ridges, handle edges, and on other irregularities in the form. This is because the glaze becomes quite thin on these particular areas. In these thin sections, the copper is volatilized and the glaze is therefore transparent and colorless. This quality of thinning on lips and edges is an attractive feature, particularly when a porcelain body is used. Any of the porcelain compositions presented in Chapter 2 on crystalline glazes will work well with copper reduction glazes when fired to cone 9.

Preparing Copper Reduction Glazes

When you prepare the glazes which follow, you should wet-grind them on a ball mill for two hours. Unground glazes lack the homogeneity necessary to create the best effects. Prepare only as much glaze as you are going to apply at the time. Most copper reduction glazes contain some soluble materials, and these will re-crystallize in the glaze if they are mixed with water and allowed to set for any length of time. In addition to re-crystallization, a change also takes place in the glazes when they are stored wet; often they will not fire exactly like freshly mixed glazes.

Reduction-Fired Copper Glaze Compositions

The copper reduction glaze compositions which follow are divided into two types. The first group includes those for which a reducing fire should be used; the second group includes localized reduction glazes to be fired in an oxidizing fire. Even though the first group consists of reduction-fired glazes, the compositions listed include silicon carbide as an aid in the reduction process.

Both types of glazes have been thoroughly tested following the schedules described at the end of this chapter: they do work, so be persistent in your effort. A brief statement concerning the reaction or color of each glaze follows its composition. Glazes III-4, IV-4, and IV-13 are listed as both reduction-fired and localized reduction glazes because extreme differences in color result when these glazes are fired under the two procedures.

In general, the glazes fired in an oxidizing atmosphere have had more predictable results than those fired in a reducing atmosphere. However, you should try both types of glazes and make your own decision as to which you find more exciting.

I-5 Copper Reduction Glaze (cone 9 – 10)

Pemco frit #P 283	2.320%
SS-65 brand sodium silicate	3.820%
Edgar plastic kaolin	9.483%
Whiting	9.183%
Zinc oxide	2.522%
Silica	26.040%
Custer keystone spar	5.471%
Borax	5.471%
Copper carbonate	.456%
Silicon carbide (FFF grain)	.334%
Tin oxide	.962%
Ferro frit #3134	4.396%
Kingman spar	27.056%
Cullet	1.986%
Bentonite	.518%
	100.00%

Note: This glaze is light red with dark red mottling.

I-6 Copper Reduction Glaze (cone 9 – 10)

Pemco frit #P 283	2.32%
SS-65 brand sodium silicate	3.80%
Edgar plastic kaolin	9.48%
Whiting	6.98%
Zinc oxide	2.79%
Silica	26.24%
Custer keystone spar	5.47%
Borax	5.47%
Copper carbonate	.46%
Silicon carbide (FFF grain)	.34%
Tin oxide	.97%
Ferro frit #3134	7.02%
Kingman spar	27.62%
Bentonite	1.04%
	100.00%

Note: This glaze is a mottled medium red.

I-9 Copper Reduction Glaze (cone 9 – 10)

Pemco #P 283	1.16%
Edgar plastic kaolin	4.74%
Whiting	7.25%
Zinc oxide	3.20%
Silica	22.66%
Custer keystone spar	2.74%
Borax	2.74%
Copper carbonate	.52%
Silicon carbide (FFF grain)	.32%
Tin oxide	.99%
Ferro frit #3134	7.91%
Kingman spar	40.86%
Cullet	1.98%
Bentonite	1.03%
SS-65 brand sodium silicate	1.90%
	100.00%

Note: This glaze is red-pink with darker red spots when fired on the schedule described for reduction firing. Good dark red when fired to cone 10 down.

I-12 Copper Reduction Glaze (cone 9 – 10)

Pemco frit #P 283	3.48%
SS-65 brand sodium silicate	5.70%
Edgar plastic kaolin	14.23%
Whiting	8.91%
Zinc oxide	2.11%
Silica	29.62%
Custer keystone spar	8.21%
Borax	8.21%
Copper carbonate	.40%
Silicon carbide (FFF grain)	.35%
Tin oxide	.94%
Ferro frit #3134	3.51%
Kingman spar	13.81%
Bentonite	.52%
	100.00%

Note: With proper reduction, produces excellent ruby red and is mottled in texture. Not mature at cone 9 touching.

I-14 Copper Reduction Glaze (cone 9 – 10)

Ferro frit #3134	11.42%
Kingman spar	54.67%
Cullet	1.99%
Whiting	5.31%
Zinc oxide	3.88%
Silica	19.27%

Copper carbonate	.57%
Silicon carbide (FFF grain)	.31%
Tin oxide	1.02%
Bentonite	1.56%
	100.00%

Note: Blood red glaze with darker red spots. A very handsome glaze.

II-7 Copper Reduction Glaze (cone 9 – 10)

Pemco frit #P 283	1.16%
SS-65 brand sodium silicate	1.90%
Edgar plastic kaolin	4.74%
Whiting	5.04%
Zinc oxide	3.47%
Silica	22.86%
Custer keystone spar	2.74%
Borax	2.74%
Copper carbonate	.52%
Silicon carbide (FFF grain)	.32%
Tin oxide	1.00%
Ferro frit #3134	10.53%
Kingman spar	41.43%
Bentonite	1.55%
	100.00%

Note: This glaze is a mottled red and pink, a crushed-strawberry color. At cone 10 down, very rich dark red.

II-12 Reduction Copper Glaze (cone 9 – 10)

Ferro frit #3134	10.53%
Kingman spar	41.43%
Whiting	3.28%
Zinc oxide	3.11%
Silica	21.96%
Bentonite	1.55%
Copper carbonate	.51%
Silicon carbide (FFF grain)	.47%
Tin oxide	1.49%
Ferro frit #3191	7.12%
Kona F4 spar	8.31%
Red iron oxide	.24%
	100.00%

Note: This glaze is a bright, very lively dark red with some mottling and streaking.

III-3 Copper Reduction Glaze (cone 9 – 10)

Ferro frit #3134	10.53%
Kingman spar	41.43%
Whiting	6.33%
Zinc oxide	3.11%
Silica	23.00%
Bentonite	1.55%
Copper carbonate	.48%
Silicon carbide (FFF grain)	.30%
Tin oxide	1.01%
Kona F4 spar	8.55%
Buckingham spar	.64%
Calcined borax	2.18%
SS-65 brand sodium silicate	.30%
Borax	.39%
Edgar plastic kaolin	.20%
	100.00%

Note: This glaze is a comparatively light red with a network of darker red spots.

III-2 Reduction Copper Glaze (cone 9 – 10)

Ferro frit #3134	10.53%
Kingman spar	41.43%
Whiting	7.07%
Zinc oxide	3.45%
Silica	25.81%
Bentonite	1.55%
Copper carbonate	.49%
Silicon carbide (FFF grain)	.29%
Tin oxide	1.08%
Ferro frit #3191	.66%
SS-65 brand sodium silicate	2.60%
Edgar plastic kaolin	2.88%
Calcined borax	2.16%
	100.00%

Note: This glaze is a light red with darker spots.

III-4 Copper Reduction Glaze (cone 9 – 10)

Ferro frit #3134	7.02%
Kingman spar	27.62%
Whiting	11.03%
Zinc oxide	2.76%
Silica	32.15%
Bentonite	1.03%
Copper carbonate	.41%
Silicon carbide (FFF grain)	.28%
Tin oxide	1.12%
Ferro frit #3191	1.31%
SS-65 brand sodium silicate	5.20%
Edgar plastic kaolin	5.75%
Calcined borax	4.32%
	100.00%

Note: This glaze is a quite rich, red-purple color, sometimes partly mottled with pale blue.

III-5 Copper Reduction Glaze (cone 9 – 10)

Kingman spar	27.62%
Ferro frit #3134	7.02%
Whiting	10.29%
Zinc oxide	2.42%
Silica	29.34%
Bentonite	1.04%
Copper carbonate	.40%
Silicon carbide (FFF grain)	.27%
Tin oxide	1.05%
Ferro frit #3191	.66%
SS-65 brand sodium silicate	2.90%
Edgar plastic kaolin	3.08%
Calcined borax	4.34%
Kona F4 spar	8.55%
Buckingham spar	.64%
Borax	.38%
	100.00%

Note: This glaze has been a repeater rather consistently. It is between a ruby and garnet red with a mottled quality. An excellent glaze.

IV-4 Copper Reduction Glaze (cone 9 – 10)

Kona F4 spar	43.80%
Whiting	12.83%
Talc	2.95%
Zinc oxide	3.30%
Edgar plastic kaolin	5.75%
Silica	22.90%
Tin oxide	.66%
Cupric oxide	.20%
Silicon carbide (FFF grain)	.29%
Calcined borax	4.13%
SS-65 brand sodium silicate	2.48%
Ferro frit #3191	.62%
Copper carbonate	.09%
	100.00%

Note: This glaze is somewhat fluid when fired in a reducing fire. It is a very smooth, yellowish pink color, with a high gloss.

Localized Reduction Copper Glaze Compositions

The following glaze compositions are to be used in an oxidizing atmosphere according to the schedule presented later. Contrary to custom, all the following localized reduction copper glazes include the coloring agent as well as the reducing agent as part of the 100% total glaze composition.

II-10 Oxidation – Copper Reduction Glaze

Pemco frit #P283	1.16%
SS-65 brand sodium silicate	1.90%
Edgar Plastic kaolin	4.74%
Whiting	5.56%
Zinc oxide	.36%
Silica	30.33%
Custer keystone spar	2.74%
Borax (calcined)	2.74%
Ferro frit #3191	21.37%
Kona F-4 spar	24.93%
Copper carbonate	.30%
Tin oxide	2.36%
Red iron oxide	.71%
Silicon carbide (FFF grain)	.80%
	100.00%

Note: This glaze is red-violet in color with white flecks throughout. It is a favorite with some potters while others do not like it at all. On a paddled form it thins on the ridges to show more red color on those areas. This color has been called magenta. A very interesting glaze.

IV-13 Copper Reduction Glaze (cone 9 – 10)

Kona F4 spar	13.76%
Silica	28.93%
Calcined borax	4.13%
Whiting	14.24%
Tin oxide	1.00%
Copper carbonate	.25%
Silicon carbide (FFF grain)	.30%
SS-65 brand sodium silicate	2.48%
Ferro frit #3191	.63%
Zinc oxide	1.95%
Ferro frit #3134	3.65%
Kona A3 spar	25.93%
Edgar plastic kaolin	2.75%
	100.00%

Note: This glaze, as well as IV-14 from the following oxidation firing group, is an excellent orchid with blue streaks.

IV-7 Copper Reduction Glaze (cone 9 – 10)

Kona F4 spar	35.67%

Whiting	14.05%
Talc	1.48%
Zinc oxide	2.00%
Edgar plastic kaolin	5.63%
Silica	29.04%
Tin oxide	.79%
Cupric oxide	.10%
Silicon carbide (FFF grain)	.23%
Copper carbonate	.14%
Calcined borax	6.19%
SS-65 brand sodium silicate	3.73%
Ferro frit #3191	.95%
	100.00%

Note: This glaze is red-pink with dark red streaks.

III-4 Oxidation Copper Reduction Glaze (cone 9)

Ferro frit #3134	7.02%
Kingman spar	27.62%
Whiting	11.03%
Zinc oxide	2.76%
Ferro frit #3191	1.31%
SS-65 brand sodium silicate	5.20%
Edgar plastic kaolin	5.75%
Calcined borax	4.31%
Silica	32.15%
Bentonite	1.04%
Copper carbonate	.41%
Silicon carbide (FFF grain)	.28%
Tin oxide	1.12%
	100.00%

Note: This glaze is a strong red-purple with flecks, almost spots, of blue-white distributed rather uniformly throughout. At one cone higher, the flecks or spots would probably become streaks.

III-7 Oxidation Copper Reduction Glaze (cone 9)

Ferro frit #3134	3.51%
Kingman spar	13.81%
Zinc oxide	2.07%
Silica	38.49%
Bentonite	.52%
Ferro frit #3191	1.97%
SS-65 brand sodium silicate	7.80%
Edgar plastic kaolin	8.63%
Calcined borax	6.47%
Copper carbonate	.32%
Silicon carbide (FFF grain)	.26%

Tin oxide	1.16%
Whiting	14.99%
	100.00%

Note: This is a pink and gray speckled glaze. The speckled quality of the color has been compared to salt and pepper. If fired about one or two cones higher, the speckles would probably become streaks. A very subdued glaze.

III-8 Oxidation Copper Reduction Glaze (cone 9)

Ferro frit #3134	3.51%
Kingman spar	13.81%
Whiting	14.25%
Zinc oxide	1.72%
Silica	35.68%
Bentonite	.52%
Copper carbonate	.31%
Silicon carbide (FFF grain)	.27%
Tin oxide	1.09%
Ferro frit #3191	1.31%
SS-65 brand sodium silicate	5.50%
Edgar plastic kaolin	5.95%
Calcined borax	6.50%
Kona F-4 spar	8.55%
Buckingham spar	.64%
Raw borax	.39%
	100.00%

Note: This glaze is blue with lavender and white streaks. The streaks are short, creating the effect of a mottled surface.

III-9 Oxidation Copper Reduction Glaze (cone 9)

Ferro frit #3134	3.50%
Kingman spar	13.81%
Whiting	13.51%
Zinc oxide	1.38%
Silica	32.87%
Bentonite	.52%
Copper carbonate	.30%
Silicon carbide (FFF grain)	.27%
Tin oxide	1.01%
Ferro frit #3191	.66%
SS-65 brand sodium silicate	3.20%
Edgar plastic kaolin	3.28%
Calcined borax	6.52%
Kona F-4 spar	17.11%
Buckingham spar	1.28%
Raw borax	.77%
	100.00%

Note: This glaze is very similar to III-4. The one difference is that this one may tend more toward blue-purple. It retains the blue-white flecks or spots.

III-10 Oxidation Copper Reduction Glaze (cone 9)

Ferro frit #3134	3.51%
Kingman spar	13.81%
Whiting	12.79%
Zinc oxide	1.04%
Silica	30.06%
Bentonite	.52%
Copper carbonate	.28%
Silicon carbide	.28%
Tin oxide	.94%
Kona F-4 spar	25.66%
Buckingham spar	1.92%
Calcined borax	6.54%
SS-65 brand sodium silicate	.89%
Raw borax	1.16%
Edgar plastic kaolin	.60%
	100.00%

Note: When fired according to the schedule which follows, this glaze will produce a very dark, red-brown glaze that is uninteresting in itself. After having fired the glaze on the pot, it is recommended that you fire it again on the same schedule. Before refiring, however, grind away the excess glaze at the foot of the piece. If you like the piece after the second firing, keep it. If you do not like the very dark color, grind the excess glaze from the lower part of the piece again and spray a coat of glaze #IV-4-0 over it. The result will be a very exciting red plum color. (Who says the Chinese meant "green plums" when they mentioned "plum" in glazes colored by copper?)

IV-3 Oxidation Copper Reduction Glaze (cone 9)

Kona F-4 spar	45.8%
Whiting	12.0%
Talc	5.0%
Zinc oxide	5.0%
Edgar plastic kaolin	6.0%
Silica	10.0%
Tin oxide	.6%
Copper carbonate	.3%
Silicon carbide (FFF grain)	.3%
Ferro frit #3134	2.0%
Eureka spar	13.0%
	100.0%

Note: This glaze is a medium pink with light pink and red streaks at cone 9. Almost identical with IV-2 when fired to cone 11 with time extended one hour on medium switch position.

IV-2 Oxidation Copper Reduction Glaze (cone 9 down, cone 10 at 3:00 o'clock)

Kona F-4 spar	51.9%
Whiting	11.7%
Talc	4.4%
Zinc oxide	4.7%
Edgar plastic kaolin	5.9%
Silica	16.7%
Calcined borax	2.1%
Pemco frit #P 283	.3%
SS-65 brand sodium silicate	1.2%
Tin oxide	.5%
Copper carbonate	.3%
Silicon carbide (FFF grain)	.3%
	100.0%

Note: This glaze is a strong, bright red with pink streaks at cone 9 down, cone 10 at 3:00 o'clock. When fired to cone 11 with the time on medium switch extended one hour, it becomes transparent and colorless at the top of the piece with red streaks on the lower portion of the pot.

IV-4 Oxidation Reduction Copper Glaze (cone 9)

Kona F-4 spar	43.8%
Whiting	12.8%
Talc	2.9%
Zinc oxide	3.3%
SS-65 brand sodium silicate	2.5%
Ferro frit #3191	.6%
Calcined borax	4.1%
Edgar plastic kaolin	5.8%
Silica	22.9%
Tin oxide	.7%
Copper carbonate	.3%
Silicon carbide (FFF grain)	.3%
	100%

Note: When applied fairly heavily, this glaze is red with pink streaks. When more thinly applied, it is a slightly brownish red at cone 9. The red with pink streaks is one of the most interesting color textures among the copper reduction glazes.

IV-7 Oxidation Copper Reduction Glaze (cone 9)

Kona F-4 spar	35.66%

Whiting	14.05%
Talc	1.48%
Zinc oxide	2.00%
SS-65 brand sodium silicate	3.73%
Ferro frit #3191	.95%
Calcined borax	6.20%
Edgar plastic kaolin	5.63%
Silica	29.04%
Tin oxide	.79%
Copper carbonate	.24%
Silicon carbide (FFF grain)	.23%
	100.00%

Note: This glaze should be applied heavily and fired to cone 9. Then any excessive thickness of glaze should be ground from around the foot and the piece should be fired a second time. Grind the excess glaze from the foot area again and spray the piece with a coat of glaze #IV-14. The result will be a very rich plum purple with an indication of blue haze or "bloom" on the surface. This glaze is a favorite of many potters.

IV-14 Oxidation Copper Reduction Glaze
(cone 9 – 10)

Kona F-4 spar	6.88%
Silica	25.78%
Calcined borax	2.06%
Whiting	13.73%
Tin oxide	1.04%
Copper carbonate	.29%
Silicon carbide (FFF grain)	.31%
SS-65 brand sodium silicate	1.24%
Ferro frit #3191	.31%
Edgar plastic kaolin	1.38%
Zinc oxide	2.60%
Ferro frit #3134	5.48%
Kona A-3 spar	38.90%
	100.00%

Note: This glaze varies between purple when thick and magenta when applied more thinly. The purple-to-magenta background displays evenly spaced blue spots on the surface of the glaze. A very unusual and handsome glaze.

EWS #11c Oxidation Copper Reduction Glaze
(cone 9 – 10)

Buckingham spar	42.0%
Colemanite	16.0%
Zinc oxide	.2%
Barium carbonate	2.0%
Talc	4.0%
Kaolin	2.0%
Whiting	5.0%
Silica	28.0%
Tin oxide	1.0%
Copper carbonate	.2%
Silicon carbide (FFF grain)	.2%
	100.0%

Note: This is another triple-fired glaze that should be treated exactly like oxidation glaze IV-7. The color is about midway between the red plum of III-10-0 and the deep plum color of IV-7-0.

IV-13 Oxidation Copper Reduction Glaze
(cone 9 – 10)

Kona F-4 spar	13.76%
Silica	28.93%
Calcined borax	4.13%
Whiting	14.24%
Tin oxide	1.00%
Copper carbonate	.25%
Silicon carbide (FFF grain)	.30%
SS-65 brand sodium silicate	2.48%
Ferro frit #3191	.63%
Edgar plastic kaolin	2.75%
Zinc oxide	1.95%
Ferro frit #3134	3.65%
Kona A-3 spar	25.93%
	100.00%

Note: A very rich reddish purple with blue spots. A very satisfactory glaze.

Applying Copper Reduction Glazes

Copper reduction glazes may be applied by spraying, dipping, or pouring. Spraying allows for greater control over the thickness of the glaze coat. There is no substitute for experience when it comes to applying any glaze, and the copper reduction glaze is no exception. In a very general way, we can say that the thickness of the glazes presented in this chapter should be between 1/32" and 1/16" in thickness. In most instances, it should be closer to 1/16" thick on the shoulders and the top part of the form, tapering to about 1/32" toward the base. Remember, however, that the color usually burns out if the glaze is too thin. Some potters find that having the body show through is a very appealing feature, while others do not like it. If you want uniform color all over the piece, make the thickness of the glaze coat as uniform as possible.

Although viscous, copper reduction glazes are fluid and will flow down the side of the piece. If you want the thick roll of glaze above the foot that is so characteristic of some Chinese pieces, scrape off all the glaze about 1/2" up from the foot and paint this area with fine powdered alumina mixed with gum tragacanth solution.

The Chinese may have used a very finely powdered charcoal for this purpose, and you might also want to try that. The action we may assume takes place is that the fluid glaze stops when it comes in contact with the residue of charcoal. The charcoal should be obtained from a material high in alumina and silica in order to provide the non-fusion necessary to stop the flow of glaze. It is very possible that the Chinese used charcoal obtained from rice hulls; rice hull ash is composed of 96% silica and 1% alumina.

If you do not like unglazed body color at the foot, you should spray a uniform coating of glaze over the entire piece and fire the piece on a pedestal with a slab under it as described for firing crystalline-glazed pieces.

Firing Copper Reduction Glazes

Any of the glazes described in this chapter will work when fired according to one of the following schedules. You will find that the schedules presented here are for a specific size and make of kiln. As you must know from experience, each individual kiln, regardless of size or make, has its own unique "personality." Whatever type of kiln you use, experiment with various firing schedules, and keep a complete record of everything you do so that you will be able to repeat each firing as closely as possible, should you wish to do so.

Reduction Firing Schedule. The reduction-fired glazes were fired in the A.D. Alpine H.F.S. #2 kiln. This is a gas-burning kiln with a two-cubic-foot ware chamber. It has one burner on each side with a single blower for forced air draft. It is an up-draft kiln with damper slabs on the top and secondary air ports around the burners in the front and on each side at the back. It has a tendency to be somewhat cooler in the front part of the ware chamber than in the back portion. This can result in some interesting variations of color, sometimes on a single piece. All the reduction-fired glaze compositions listed have produced satisfactory results when fired in the kiln, on the following schedule.

1. 1 hour, on pilot burners alone, 340°F. (170°C.).

2. 1 hour, retain pilot flame, plus gas 1/4, plus air 20, plus 1" damper opening, 640°F. (340°C.).

3. 1 hour, retain pilot flame, plus gas 1/2, plus air 30, plus 1" damper opening, 1180°F. (about 640°C.).

4. 4 hours, pilots off, plus gas 2, plus air 40, plus 1 1/2" damper opening, from 1300°F. to 1980°F. (from 700° to 1080°C.).

5. 1/2 hour, pilots off, plus gas 3, plus air 60, plus 1 1/2" damper opening, 2000°F. (1095°C.).

6. 1 1/2 to 1 3/4 hours, blower 1/2 covered, plus gas 6 3/4, air 80, plus 1 1/2" damper opening, 2180°F. (1195°C.).

7. Reduction. 1 hour blower covered 3/4, plus gas 6 3/4, plus air 100, plus 1/2" damper opening. Start reduction when cone 8 down, cone 9 at 3:00 o'clock. Secondary air ports closed in back of kiln until reduction starts, then opened.

8. Oxidation. 45 to 50 minutes blower uncovered, plus gas 3, plus air 60, plus 1" damper opening.

Temperatures vary with thermocouples in various kilns, and mechanical devices are never as dependable as pyrometric cones. Do not be afraid to experiment with firing schedules in your kiln. A longer and hotter fire may be advantageous; a total of 15 to 18 hours to cone 10 or even 11 may work well for some glazes. When cone 9 is at 3:00 o'clock at the start of the one-hour reduction period, cone 10 may be at 3:00 o'clock or touching when the kiln is turned off.

Localized Reduction Firing Schedule

Baggs and Littlefield (see Bibliography) recommend a 24-hour firing period, using an oxidizing fire, in a gas-fired down-draft kiln with a 24-cubic-foot capacity. The 24 hours does not include the cooling period.

Procedure A. When working with localized reduction glazes, Dwayne Bentzien has found that a 26 1/3 hour firing period produces superior results (see Bibliography).

1. Increase temperature approximately 100°F. (40°C.) per hour until the kiln reaches 1800°F. (980°C.).

2. Increase temperature approximately 50°F. (10°C.) per hour between 1800°F. and 2100°F. (980° and 1150°C.).

3. The final portion of the firing period is more rapid, with an approximate increase of 150°F.

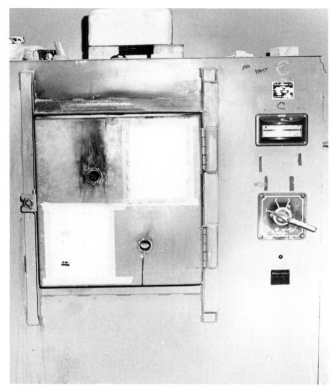

The Alpine Electric Globar kiln model E.F.G. #3, with maximum operating temperature of 3000°F. (1149°C.), is used for firing both crystalline and localized copper reduction glazes.

(70°C.) per hour until 2350°F. (1290°C.) has been reached.

This represents a firing period of 25 hours, 40 minutes. The kiln should be turned off at 2350°F. (1290°C.) and cooled normally at approximately 150°F. (70°C.) per hour.

The kiln Bentzien used was approximately 10 cubic feet in capacity. It had glo-bar heating elements controlled by a panel of eight knife switches which could be set in 10 switching positions. This kiln provides an unusual degree of temperature control.

Procedure B. However, most studios do not have a kiln of this complexity, and the localized reduction glazes were fired in an A.D. Alpine E.F.G. #3 electric kiln (208 volts, 39 amps, 14 KW). This kiln has glo-bar elements and a three-position switch. It will reach a temperature of 3000°F. (1650°C.), so there is no danger of over-firing refractories. The schedule used for firing the localized reduction was as follows.

1. 2 hours (room temp. to 700°F., 320°C.).

2. 8 hours (700°F. to 1840°F., 320° to 1000°C.).

3. 2 to 2½ hours till cone 9 down. Cone 10 touching, 2360+°F., (1290+°C.). The firing cycle totals 12½ hours. This is very much shorter than the firing schedule for either the Baggs and Littlefield study or the Bentzien study.

Glazes fired in this manner have an orange-peel texture. If you find this objectionable you can obtain a higher gloss and eliminate the orange-peel texture by re-firing the piece on the same firing schedule. If the piece has a sufficiently heavy coating of glaze, color can often be intensified by a second firing. If the glaze coat is too thin, the color may be lost during a second firing.

Try variations on this firing schedule, such as a longer firing period and hotter temperatures, to create other interesting effects.

Defects Resulting from Firing

Too short a firing cycle or not enough heat or a combination of both will cause a copper reduction glaze to become a mass of blisters, a muddy gray-brown color or a rather unpleasant reddish brown color. If you see evidence of any of these effects when you take a piece from the kiln, you may assume that one of the following events occurred during firing. The blistered glaze is immature. The kiln was either turned off before the maturing temperature had been reached or fired to maturing temperature too rapidly. Copper reduction glazes go through a rather violent boiling period during the firing process. Blistered pots occur when the process is stopped in the middle; the kiln is turned off and the glazes remain in a blistered condition as they cool.

Muddy gray-brown colored pots result from localized reduction when they are not fired long enough or to a high enough temperature to permit the carborundum to be used up. Reduced copper, unreduced copper, and carborundum are all suspended in the glaze at the same time. If you obtain a gray-black muddy brown in a reducing fire, it means that there is unused carborundum in the glaze or that there has been too much smoke in the kiln and the gray black color has been created by carbon entrapped in the glaze. This is a sign of poor reduction technique.

A brown glaze indicates under-firing or too short a firing period. Reduced copper, which is red, and probably the sub-oxide of copper (Cu_4O), which is olive green, create the brown color. Prolonging the firing will give the Cu_4O a chance to become colloidal copper, and the resulting color will be red.

A transparent, colorless glaze may mean one of two things. First, the glaze coat may have been too thin and the copper, which is very volatile at high temperatures, may have been lost from the glaze. The copper may have volatilized in a reducing fire, but it is more likely that the copper is still there. There is such a small amount of copper in a reduction glaze that when there is over-oxidation at the end of the firing cycle, the copper very often changes back to CuO; this produces such a pale blue color that it is not visible on a porcelain body. Sometimes it is possible to send an over-oxidized pot through another reduction fire and obtain red. Most often, however, it is advisable to give it another coat of glaze before re-firing.

This piece displays an immature copper red glaze. More heat and longer fire would smooth out the surface and produce a mature glaze.

*The semi-matte iron red ash glaze
used on this piece by Leonard Burch
consists of Buckingham Spar 40,
Kentucky Ball Clay 20, Oak Ash 40,
and Red Iron Oxide 10.*

Wood Ash and Plant Ash Glazes

Wood ash and plant ash are composed of oxides of the various elements commonly found in glazes, the most important of which are the oxides of sodium, potassium, calcium, alumina, and silica. In many instances, the proportions of these oxides found naturally in wood or plant ash are such that when the ash is applied to a clay body and fired to cone 9 or 10, they form a glaze. These glazes have either a matte or a bright, high-gloss surface, depending on the ash used. An ash such as pine or cypress, that has a high proportion of sodium, potassium, and calcium and a low proportion of alumina and silica is considered soft ash. As the proportions of alumina and particularly of silica increase, as they do in oat straw ash, the ash is referred to as medium. With a still greater increase in the proportion of these elements, as there is in fern ash, the ash is considered hard, or refractory. Another classification could be made — that of extra hard — for rice hulls, which produce ash that is approximately 96% to 99% silica.

Because the composition of wood and plant ash varies depending on the season and the area in which they grow, the results of using the same kind of ash will vary from one location and from one season to another. However, the use of wood and plant ash of any composition will lead to interesting results that are not otherwise obtainable.

Collecting and Preparing Ash Material

Ash that is satisfactory for use in glazes can be secured in many ways. If you live in an area where orchards are pruned every year, it may be a very simple matter for you to get ash when the pruned wood is burned. If, however, you must rely upon your own resources and you have no wooded area of your own, try to secure permission from the owner of the nearest woods to collect fallen leaves, branches, bark, or possibly a whole fallen tree. Under some trees, such as eucalyptus and sycamore, you can always find pieces of bark which have fallen on the ground around them; lawn clippings and hedge prunings are always available, and all kinds of weeds can be used. The leaves, bark, twigs, branches, and heartwood you collect will probably differ from one another in composition; it is also probable that the compositions of the leaves and twigs will vary from spring to fall, as will those of the weeds.

Try to collect a large supply of ash materials at one time, so that you will have a large enough quantity of ash to continue working with one particular glaze composition. Keep a record of where and when you collect your material and exactly what it is — leaves, bark, weeds, and so on.

When you have collected a large pile of material, you will be ready to burn it. Burning should be done on a large, clean area of hard-packed earth; a clean fireplace is also an ideal area to burn materials. If you have no such place, you can make a burner by removing the top of a large oil drum and cutting a hole about 8″ square near the bottom of the drum to provide draft. You can make a rack or grate by cutting a piece of expanded metal (a commercial product which looks like a heavy wire mesh) to fit snugly inside the drum. The rack should be supported inside the drum by four bricks placed on end in the bottom of the drum. Begin by burning the smaller, more delicate pieces and save the heavier material for when the fire is well underway. You will find that a great pile of material makes only a small amount of ash, but then you can always make more.

Chinese Procedure for Preparing Ash

The following is Japanese potter Kenkichi Tomimoto's explanation of the procedure used by the Chinese to prepare the ash which when mixed with feldspar produces their characteristic high-temperature glazes.

"The Chinese would prepare bracken [fern] in a great pile about ten meters by thirty meters, until it was about one meter high, then weight it down with slabs of limestone. This would press it down to about half a meter, then another meter of bracken weighted down with limestone and so on until they had a stack of alternate layers of bracken and limestone about two meters high. Then they would burn it. The resulting mixture of bracken ash and calcium was ground on an ox mill and used as ash, the ash was then mixed with feldspar and used as a glaze. The proportions were 10 parts by volume feldspar to 12 parts by volume ash."

Origin of Ash Glazing in Japan

A number of different kinds of ash are used by potters in Japan. Some of them are: Isu wood ash, pine wood ash, rice-hull ash, bamboo ash, rice-straw ash, common ash (a mixture), oak wood ash, and camphor wood ash. However, no one knows how wood ash first came to be used as a glaze material in Japan. The practice may have been imported from China by way of Korea or it may have been an accidental discovery. The following argument for accidental discovery is very strong.

All primitive Japanese ware was soft and unglazed. Not until the Ana-gama (cellar kiln) was developed was it possible to reach temperatures high enough to make the ware hard and durable. The structure of the Ana-gama was such that it would reach temperatures as high as cone 9 or cone 10. The ware was stacked one piece on top of another in it, and triangular, wedge-shaped pads of clay called "tochi" (pillows) were used to keep each stack of ware upright on the sloping floor (about 30° slope). Sometimes the ware was stacked like cordwood, which accounts for much of the distortion of form in the old Bizen, Tamba, Shigaraki, and Tokoname wares. As each piece started to vitrify, the weight of the pieces stacked on top of it caused its wall to sag and sometimes caused several pieces to stick together. This condition of vitrification, or incipient glassiness, of the body was an important feature in accidental glazing. The fuel for the kiln was either cypress or pine wood, both of which produce a soft, light-weight ash. Each time the kiln was stoked, ash was caught up by the draft, flew through the firing chamber, fell onto the tacky surface of the vitrifying ware, and stuck fast. With continued increase in temperature, the oxides in the ash fused with the silica and alumina in the clay to form a glaze. As the firing progressed, more ash settled on the ware, causing the glaze to thicken and often to run down the piece.

Today in Bizen, the more modern kilns are manipulated during the firing process to promote what is called the "falling-ash glaze" effect; although the glaze coat is not usually as thick, this effect resembles the accidental glazing that naturally occurred on ware fired in an Ana-gama.

Falling-Ash Glazing Procedure

A 20th-century Japanese potter, Rosanjin, has fired imitations, or copies of old Shigaraki and old Tamba ware in a Nobori-gama. He used the following process, which you could also use to create a falling-ash glaze effect on your ware.

Stoneware bodies that fire red or brown are usually more attractive when glazed by this process than are the lighter-colored clays; large, massive, freely thrown pieces lend themselves well to a falling-ash glazing.

Throw the form so that it needs no trimming. As soon as the form is thrown, sift a layer about 1/8" thick of pine or cypress ash onto the shoulder of the piece. Allow some ash to fall part-way down the side, but be sure this area is thinner than the layer on the shoulder. The piece can be fired as soon as it is dry. Fire to cone 9 or cone 10 in either an oxidizing or reducing fire.

If you have a biscuited piece that you feel would profit from this glazing technique, spray or paint a thick coat of gum tragacanth solution on the areas where you want glaze, then sift ash onto the wet gum coating, dry, and fire.

Complex Ash Glazes

More sophisticated ash glazes can be made by combining ash with other materials. The table at the end of this chapter lists the results obtained by combining prune and apricot (fruitwood) ashes, walnut ash, and oat-straw (grain) ash with some common ceramic materials. As you will see, the reactions of the various feldspars with ash are quite similar to one another. When used with feldspar — or a combination of feldspar and clay — most wood ashes produce a matte-glaze with varying fluidity.

Also listed are the results obtained by firing these ashes alone; these results indicate that the combination prune and walnut wood glazes may be classified as hard, the fruitwood ash glazes as soft, and the oat-straw glaze as medium. With the exception of the glazes in which ash alone was used, the compositions include 50% ash and 50% other material. All glazes listed were fired to cone 9 in an oxidizing atmosphere to obtain the results described.

Garden-weed Ash Glaze Compositions

Additional experiments have been conducted using garden-weed ash from a garden incinerator. The composition included garden weeds and shrub and lawn clippings, as well as squash vines, berry bushes, and a variety of flower stalks. Approximately 10% of garden soil was included in the composition. This conglomerate mixture yielded a glaze of medium hardness. When fired alone, the mixture produced a light, cream gray matte; with a granular texture when thinly applied.

The following glazes were fired to cone 9 in an oxidizing atmosphere on a stoneware with a high percentage of grog.

G.W. #12 Ash Glaze (cone 9)

Garden weed ash	50%
Pyrophyllite	50%
Bentonite	3% by addition

Note: A non-fluid brown matte with an almost-rough, pebbled, completely fused surface.

G.W. #13 Ash Glaze (cone 9)

Garden weed ash	50%
Nepheline syenite	50%
Bentonite	3% by addition

*This mesembryanthemum ash glaze
is composed of
50% ash and 50% Kona A3 feldspar.*

Note: Excellent, light gray transparent matte with velvet texture when thickly applied, sugary texture when thin.

G.W. #17 Ash Glaze (cone 9)

Garden weed ash	50%
Custer feldspar	50%
Copper carbonate	2% by addition

Note: Brilliant, glossy, gun-metal green with iridescence.

K #9 Ash Glaze (cone 9)

Kelp ash	50%
Nepheline syenite	50%
Bentonite	3% by addition

Note: Crystalline, creamy matte with silvery reflections.

E.A. #5 Ash Glaze (cone 9)

Eucalyptus ash	50%
Nepheline syenite	50%
Calcined kaolin	10% by addition

Note: Transparent, light tan semi-matte with excellent fish-roe crackle. This glaze may be applied to the following body and fired to cone 9.

VS #1 Vitreous Stoneware Body (cone 9)

Garden city clay	50.00%
Custer feldspar	17.00%
Silica	12.50%
Edgar plastic kaolin	9.00%
Kentucky ball clay #4	7.50%
Talc #2	3.50%
Bentonite	1.50% by addition

Note: At cone 9, this body is quite vitreous. When this body is used for slip decoration with 10% red iron oxide added, the result is a rich, golden brown to dark chestnut color under the glaze.

Additional work with eucalyptus ash and the various feldspathic materials has resulted in excessively fluid, badly crazed glazes. The addition of 15% Jordan clay to these glazes produced pleasant matte textures, all of which were tan to gray in color. The Jordan clay also corrected the excessive fluidity and in many instances eliminated the crazing entirely.

Plastic Vitrox and Ash Glaze Compositions

The results of work with plastic vitrox as an addition to garden-weed ash glazes is worth presenting here. Plastic vitrox is a plastic vitreous clay with the following composition: .045 CaO, .058 MgO, .054 Na_2O, .842 K_2O, 1.693 Al_2O_3, .005 Fe_2O_3, 14.634 SiO_2. The first three glazes in the following list use plastic vitrox in combination with eucalyptus ash. Success with this combination has prompted experimentation with plastic vitrox and apricot ash, as well as plastic vitrox and prune ash glazes. These combinations yield results similar to those of the vitrox and eucalyptus combinations — that is, crazing is eliminated, fluidity is reduced, and matteness decreases. Some of the glazes produced are comparable in color and texture to many Chinese glazes of the Sung Dynasty. All the following glaze compositions should be fired to cone 9 on stoneware clay.

P.V. 17a Ash Glaze (cone 9)

Plastic vitrox	50%
Eucalyptus ash	50%

Note: When fired on stoneware clay, this combination produces a transparent amber glaze with very high gloss and no crazing.

GL GMc Ash Glaze (cone 9)

Plastic vitrox	80%
Eucalyptus ash	15%
Jordan clay	5%

Note: This combination results in an opaque, medium-gloss, cream white, very viscous glaze that is very fat in nature. When applied thinly, it fuses completely, although the result is somewhat sugary in texture. There is no crazing, but it displays a tendency to crawl when applied too thickly.

GL G-17ek Ash Glaze (cone 9)

Plastic vitrox	55%
Eucalyptus ash	30%
Calcined kaolin	15%

Note: The result of this combination is a semi-transparent, light tan semi-matte when fired under the same conditions as the previous two glazes. There is no evidence of crazing.

GL C17a Ash Glaze (cone 9)

Plastic vitrox	50%
Prune ash	50%

Note: Opalescent, smooth-textured semi-matte with no bubbles or crazing.

GL C17a Ash Glaze (cone 9)

Plastic vitrox	80%
Prune ash	15%
Jordan clay	5%

Note: Very viscous, waxy, creamy white semi-gloss.

GL 17e Ash Glaze (cone 9)

Plastic vitrox	55%
Prune ash	30%
Raw kaolin	15%

Note: Viscous, light tan, semi-transparent glaze of medium gloss with many floating particles or bubbles submerged in the glaze. No evidence of crazing.

GL CL 7ek Ash Glaze (cone 9)

Plastic vitrox	55%
Prune ash	30%
Calcined kaolin	15%

Note: Viscous, opaque, creamy white glaze with semi-gloss and no crazing.

GL D17d Ash Glaze (cone 9)

Plastic vitrox	90%
Apricot ash	10%

Note: Sugary, white, non-fluid, semi-matte glaze with no crazing.

GL D17e Ash Glaze (cone 9)

Plastic vitrox	55%
Apricot ash	30%
Raw kaolin	15%

Note: Very pale green, transparent, high-gloss glaze with submerged seeds or bubbles. The glaze shows no indication of flowing from the piece.

Other Materials Used in Ash Glazes

Experimentation with rice-straw and beanstalk ash glazes has also been conducted. The ash of these plants may be classed as extra hard. A composition of rice-straw ash, feldspar, and clay produces a very viscous, pale lavender glaze when fired at cone 10 in an oxidizing fire. This glaze very closely re-

The bowl was glazed with 50% ash, 50% feldspar, the vase with 50% ash and 50% nepheline syenite, with 8% red iron oxide added for color.

TABLE OF COMPLEX ASH GLAZES

	Prune Wood Ash	Prune Wood Ash and Walnut Wood Ash	Apricot Wood Ash	Oat-Straw Ash
Ash Used Alone	Chestnut brown matte where thin	Non-fused brown that can be easily separated from the body of the ware	Greenish cream matte where thin; gray-green tan, waxy, semi-matte where thick	Transparent yellow-green high gloss where thin; does not fuse completely where thick
Custer Keystone Feldspar	Crackled, transparent, high-gloss where thin; pale, cream-gray matte where thick	Yellow-brown and cream, slightly fluid matte where thin; yellow with alternating matte and gloss where thick	Tan matte where thin; yellow-gray, highly fluid matte where thick	Creamy, non-fluid, semi-matte that can be used in various thicknesses as decoration
Oxford Feldspar	Alternating matte and high-gloss surface where thin; milky white matte where thick	Identical to those obtained with Custer Keystone Feldspar	Yellowish tan to gray matte when thin; gray, silky textured matte where thick	Semi-transparent semi-matte where thin; opaque, creamy white semi-matte where thick
Kona F4 Feldspar	Bluish gray, semi-transparent matte where thin; transparent, yellowish gloss where thick	Cream semi-matte where thin; yellow-gray matte where thick	Fluid gray matte with yellow-brown crystalline formations where thin	Transparent high gloss where thin; pale blue-gray semi-matte where thick
Nepheline Syenite	Yellow-brown and gray mottled matte with consistent texture whether thick or thin	Cream matte where thin; pools of crazed, transparent glass at bottom of bowls when thick	Gray-green, waxy matte with a tendency to crystallize where thick	Waxy, violet-gray, non-fluid semi-matte
Buckingham Feldspar	Transparent gloss where thin; fluid, cream gray matte where thick	Waxy, cream gray, semi-transparent semi-matte	Pearl-gray matte with silky texture	Yellow to cream matte where thin; buff gray, waxy matte where thick
Eureka Feldspar	High-gloss mottling on matte surface when thin; yellow and gray matte when thick	Identical to results obtained with nepheline syenite	Viscous, creamy-gray matte with silky texture	Opaque, pale yellow, non-fluid semi-matte
Lepidolite	Gray and brown mottled matte	Gray-brown fluid matte with greenish overcast	Gray and brown mottled, crystalline-type glaze	Grayish tan with floating cream white dots
Cornwall (Cornish) Stone	Waxy, bluish, slightly fluid matte, transparent when thin	Yellow gray matte	Fluid grayish blue and tan matte; glossy when thin	Semi-transparent, milky blue-gray, waxy semi-matte
Spodumene	Waxy, bluish-olive, fine-textured matte	Pale green, slightly fluid matte	Fluid, creamy greenish-gray matte; consistent whether thick or thin	Non-fluid, brown and green mottled semi-matte; predominantly brown when thin
Dolomite	Partly fused, sandpaper-like surface	Non-fused surface	Non-fused surface	Yellow-brown matte and gloss
Kingman Feldspar	Non-fluid, yellowish tan matte with velvety texture	Creamy gray, fine-mesh, crackled matte	Non-fluid, pale gray-green matte with silky texture	Non-fluid, waxy, cream white matte with silky texture

sembles the thick, bubbly, opalescent glazes applied to the Chun wares of the Sung Dynasty. Redwood ash has also been used in various combinations with other materials. The performance of redwood ash indicates that it may be classified as very soft; redwood may be used as a satisfactory substitute for cypress or pine ash in falling-ash glazes. Probably the most interesting glaze resulting from the use of redwood ash is the gray-tan, very fat, viscous somewhat opalescent, waxy semi-matte produced when the following composition is fired to cone 9 on stoneware clay.

RA 27 Redwood Ash Glaze (cone 10)

Redwood ash	100 pbw
Nepheline syenite	10
Kaolin	5
Boric acid	5
Rutile	5
Antimony oxide	5

Limited experimentation has been done introducing coloring oxides into ash glazes, the results of which yield glazes with rather unique qualities. If you are interested, you may find this an exciting field of exploration.

Low-Temperature Ash Glazes

The use of ash as a material in low-temperature glazes (those fired between cone 06 and cone 02) is a comparably untouched field, and exploration of the possibilities in this area are virtually unlimited. In order to be called an ash glaze, a low-temperature mixture should contain not less than 50% ash. To this may be added such materials as lead carbonate or lead oxide, borax, boric acid, soda ash, colemanite, cryolite, and lithium carbonate, all of which have comparatively low fusion points and may be used in varying amounts.

Another experiment that may produce interesting results is to use the various commercial frits in combination with ash as low-temperature glazes. Again, the possibilities in this area are unlimited. Some frits with low melting points are O. Hommel frits #71, #33, #K3, and #25, the Pemco frits P545, P700, and Ferro frit #5301. One or several of these frits used in combination with ash should produce some interesting results. Other materials may, of course, be added to the frit and ash combination. For example, the use of tin oxide and titanium dioxide in such a glaze may add great interest and increase the variety of effects possible.

Close-up of a crystal pattern.

COLOR PLATES

The variety of brilliant colors and the rich and startling effects that the glazes in this book will produce can be seen in the color plates that follow. Whenever possible, the glaze composition used on the piece and the schedule on which it was fired are given, although due to the element of chance involved, these will not necessarily always produce the same results.

All pieces are by the author unless otherwise indicated. The photographs are by John Bobeda except for the two on page 81, which are by Fred Gaeden.

Crystalline-glazed piece illustrates Crystal Frit Glaze A-7 with iron oxide.

Piece illustrates glaze made from crystal frits LM (50%) and #2 (50%) with 2% manganese oxide and 11% uranium oxide.

Crystalline-glazed piece illustrates Commercial Frit Glaze #1 with cobalt, manganese, and iron.

Covered jar illustrates use of crystal frits with copper oxide.

Piece illustrates Crystal Frit Glaze A-7 with nickel oxide.

Large covered jar glazed with a combination of crystal frits colored with copper oxide and iron oxide.

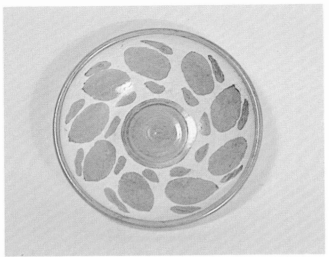

Arabian Luster Glaze R.T.-12, colored with pigment 3 and fired on schedule IV-2, results in a gold luster with abalone-shell iridescence.

Arabian Luster Glaze R.T.-12, colored with pigment 3-3 and fired on schedule IV-4-a-1, results in a gold luster on mottled gray, with red-violet reflections.

Arabian Luster Glaze R.T.-12, colored with pigment 5 and fired on schedule IV-3, results in a burnt orange and gold luster.

Arabian Luster Glaze R.T.-12, colored with pigment 4 and fired on schedule IV-4a-1, results in an old rose luster with violet reflections.

Arabian Luster Glaze R.T.-12, colored with pigment 3 and fired on schedule IV-4, results in a bright gold luster.

Arabian Luster Glaze R.T.-12, colored with pigment 2-2 and fired on schedules IV-4b and IV-4a-1, results in a red luster with ruby reflections.

Arabian Luster Glaze T.A.L., colored with pigment T.L.3 and fired on schedule IV-4-c, results in a gold and violet-gold luster.

Arabian Luster Glaze T.A.L., colored with pigment 2-2 and fired on schedule IV-4a-1, results in a light red luster with red-violet and gold reflection.

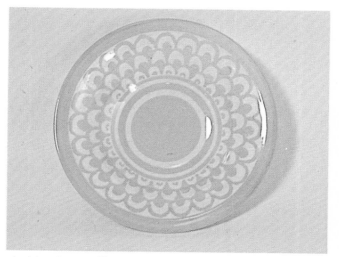

Arabian Luster Glaze T.A.L., colored with pigment 3-3 and fired on schedule T.R. 3, results in a canary yellow luster.

Arabian Luster Glaze T.A.L., colored with pigment 3-3a and fired on schedule T.R. 2, results in an orange-gold luster with iridescence.

Arabian Luster Glaze T.A.L., painted by Robert Johnson and colored with pigment 3 was fired on schedule T.R. 4, resulting in a canary yellow luster.

Arabian Luster Glaze T.A.L., painted by Robert Johnson and colored with pigment 5 was fired on schedule T.R. 2, resulting in a gold luster.

Hugh Aanonsen's crystalline-glazed piece illustrates commercial crystal frit glaze #13.

This piece by Hugh Aanonsen illustrates commercial crystal frit glaze #12.

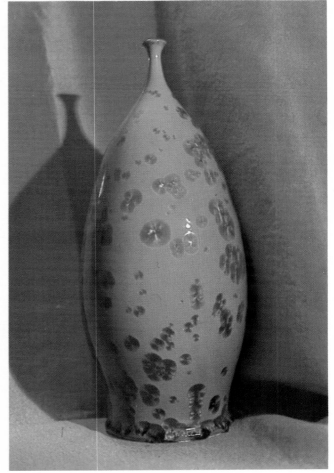

Two crystalline-glazed bottles by Hugh Aanonsen illustrate Commercial Frit Glaze #12 (left) and #19 (right).

Detail from the luster glaze demonstration shown on pages 97–99.

*This bowl by Robert E. Johnson was coated
with Tin Enamel Luster Glaze R.T.-12
and pigment TL4 and fired on Schedule TR 2
to produce its matt gold quality.*

Luster Ware

The term "overglaze decoration" means decoration on top of, or over, the fired glaze and includes the techniques of enameling and applying overglaze colors as well as applying metal over the fired glaze to create the luster effects we will discuss in this chapter. Today there are three techniques available for the production of luster ware. The smoked Arabian and liquid gold luster techniques have been used, with various modifications, for hundreds of years; the flash luster technique is the newest, having first been publicized in the early 1900s, and represents a departure from the traditional overglaze process.

Origin of Luster Ware

Overglaze decorating practices may have originated with either the Chinese or Islamic potters. In his book *A Guide to the Islamic Pottery of the Near East* (see Bibliography), Hobson expresses the opinion that "the use of enamels on the glaze seems to have developed in Persia earlier than in China." Regardless of the origin of overglaze decoration, we know that luster techniques were carried to a very high degree of perfection on early Chinese, Islamic, and Turkish pottery, as well as on many later European wares.

The earliest known example of luster ware is a small bowl of Roman-Egyptian origin, which is glazed with an alkaline copper-blue glaze with mottled areas, or flashing, of ruby red luster. The piece was found at Fostat (Old Cairo) in Egypt and is ascribed to the 3rd century A.D. The general appearance of the flashing on this piece indicates that the ruby red luster was accidental, while the Persian lusters show control of the technique and deliberate planning in regard to its placement. It is certain that the Roman-Egyptian piece bears only slight relationship to the later, highly developed luster of the Islamic pottery of Rhages in northern Persia, of Samarra on the Tigris, and of Rakka on the Euphrates in Syria, where luster production seems to have been continuous from the 9th to the 17th century.

From Spain, the luster technique spread to Italy, where it was extremely popular during the late 15th and early 16th centuries. Many of the fine luster pieces were of great interest and value to the aristocracy of that period, and there are records among Spanish legal papers indicating that luster bowls were part of an inheritance from the estate of a grandee, or Spanish, nobleman.

With the changing times, the popularity of luster ware gradually waned and the technique was replaced by the more durable polychromatic majolica — the richly colored, enameled pottery of the Italian Renaissance — which was without luster. The fall of the city-state type of government in Italy deprived Italian potters of their protectors and wealthy patrons, and the production of luster ware came to an end in that country. In Spain, this transition may have been the result of the overthrow of the Moorish rulers and the subsequent religious opposition to all persons and articles of Moorish extraction at the time of the Inquisition, which also brought about the expulsion of all Moorish people from that country. In the eastern Mediterranean, the influence of Turkish and Chinese ceramic products seems to have been sufficiently strong to have replaced the earlier luster ware by the end of the 17th century; although some luster ware was produced after that time, it was inferior in quality.

Development of Luster Techniques

During the height of its popularity, the Persian or Islamic potters were responsible for the perfection of luster decoration; this may have been the result of an effort to produce an inexpensive substitute for gold and silver wares. As mentioned earlier, this technique involves depositing a very thin layer of metal on the surface of the fired glaze. The thin deposit of metal not only produces a color but in many instances creates multicolored reflections as well.

The luster wares made by the potters of Persia and Italy, as well as those of Spain while it was under Moorish domination, have found a lasting place among the world's art treasures. Because their technique of overglaze decoration is somewhat complicated and quite beautiful in its results, its esthetic appeal is surpassed by no other method. The luster technique therefore remains a legitimate decorating process for use on glazed surfaces, and it has been employed by both Near Eastern and Western potters for centuries.

Smoked Arabian Luster Ware

The early Islamic, Hispano-Moresque, and Italian lusters, which Binns refers to as "smoked Arabian lusters" in his *The Manual of Practical Potting* (see Bibliography), were produced by first firing the glaze on the surface of the ware. After this, the metallic luster pigments were applied in the form of a paste or paint. The ware was then fired to a dull red heat, after which it was strongly reduced by the introduction of carbonaceous material into the fire box or kiln chamber. The reducing atmosphere was frequently maintained until the kiln had cooled. After firing, the pigment was washed

Bowl coated with glaze RT-12 and pigment TL 3,
fired on schedule TR 2 to produce a gold luster.

*This bowl was glazed very loosely
with a gold luster decoration
on a red and gray background.*

from the glaze surface, leaving a thin metallic film on the areas where the paste had been applied.

The Persian lusters varied in color and were predominantly either brown, olive green, greenish brown, blood red with ruby reflection, golden luster, or golden brown with ruby reflections. The most famous Hispano-Moresque luster varied from light yellow gold to red gold in color, while the ruby lusters of Gubbio were the best known in Italy.

Bodies and Glazes for Arabian Lusters

The procedure for producing smoked Arabian lusters involves using a tin-bearing glaze that provides a satisfactory white or creamy white background upon which the desired luster colors can then be developed. The glaze should mature between cone 07 and 04 and should be used on an earthenware type body — a low-fire red body and a low-fire white body — both of which mature at between cone 06 and cone 04, have also been used successfully. Although results cannot be guaranteed, porcelain bodies and bodies with only a slight iron content have also worked successfully.

Regardless of the body composition, the glaze is the most important factor in determining the effectiveness of the luster pigment during the firing process. Tin-bearing glazes containing both lead and soda seem to produce the best results. Keep in mind, however, that the presence of too great a lead content may result in reduction of the lead during the luster fire, causing the lead to turn black or gray. While not in the spirit of the original pieces, this reduction of the lead is considered by many to add to, rather than to detract from, the appeal of the ware.

The glaze must become slightly molten at a low temperature in order to accept the metallic deposit; however, too great a degree of fluidity will cause the entire luster pigment content to adhere to the surface of the glaze, producing a brown to black pattern with a sandpaper texture that is not only unpleasant but also defeats the purpose of the process.

Luster pigments can also be used effectively on a transparent glaze that contains lead and feldspar. The transparent glaze may be glost fired from cone 04 to cone 02. When fired to cone 04, the lead in the glaze is much more apt to be reduced to a dark gray or black during the decorating fire than it is when glost fired to cone 02. The lusters that can be produced on transparent glazes are gold, maroon, light red, brown, amber, orange, green, and canary yellow in color. The interesting effect of gold on a black matte results when a transparent glaze is glost fired to cone 04, decorated with pigments T3 and T4, and fired on decorating firing schedule IV-4-C, as described in this chapter.

Applying Arabian Luster Glazes

We frequently associate decoration added on top of a glaze with a thick glaze coat. However, although luster is an overglaze decoration, a thick glaze coat is not desirable with either of the glazes. Both compositions should be applied in what would be considered a thin coat. If at all possible, spray the glazes on low-fire clay biscuited to cone 04; when dipped or poured, the glazes tend to crawl during the glost fire. After glazing, the pieces should dry for 24 hours before being glost fired.

Arabian Luster Glaze Compositions

Glazes containing both lead and alkaline materials work well for the smoked Arabian lusters. While I have never tried purely alkaline-base glazes, I do believe they should also perform satisfactorily. However, to be most successful, they should probably contain some tin oxide.

The two glazes that seem to work best for Arabian luster are the R.T.-12 and T.A.L. listed here. The R.T.-12 is an opaque tin enamel and is the more difficult of the two to use. Since it contains a fairly large amount of raw borax, it should be ground in a ball mill or mortar until it is quite smooth — not grainy. Use the most finely powdered borax you can find, and mix all materials thoroughly before adding water. If the borax is not thoroughly mixed with the other materials before water is added, it will heat and cake before you can finish mixing it into a glaze slip. After adding water, grind the mixture in a ball mill or mortar until it passes through a 60-mesh screen.

The T.A.L. glaze contains no borax; the alkaline part of the glaze is in the feldspar. This glaze does not require as much grinding as the R.T.-12 glaze. Grind the glaze only until smooth, then screen it through a 60-mesh screen, and it is ready for use.

R.T.-12 Tin Enamel Luster Glaze (cone 06)

Litharge	46.65 pbw
Powdered borax	275.40
Edgar plastic kaolin	120.40
Silica	57.40
Tin oxide	55.00

Note: This glaze should not be fired above cone 06. When fired in a kiln containing chromium, this glaze will take on a chrome-tin pink color.

T.A.L. Transparent Luster Glaze (cone 04 – 02)

White lead	71.0 pbw
Whiting	12.5
Kona A3 feldspar	41.5
Calcined kaolin	6.5
Silica	22.5
Zinc oxide	2.0

Note: When this glaze is fired to cone 02 before the luster pigments are applied, there is less reduction of the lead during the subsequent luster fire, and the lusters obtained are superior.

Preparing Luster Patterns

Decorating may be done by one of two processes, depending on the result desired. If you want a free, loose decoration, you can paint it on free-hand, without first laying out a pattern. If you prefer a perfectly symmetrical pattern, lay it out carefully on the glazed surface before starting to paint with the pigment. The pattern layout may be done using either a very soft lead pencil or a small pen with a felt or bamboo point. If you use a felt pen, be sure to remove all lines not covered by pigment before you fire the piece; sometimes the ink does not burn out completely, and the lines are faintly visible after firing.

Luster Pigments

All luster pigments are basically composed of earth substances; to these are added the materials that produce the luster. The earth substances used are yellow ochre, burnt umber, and burnt sienna, all of which are composed entirely or at least partly of iron oxide and manganese. The iron and manganese present in these substances seem to play an important role in the way the pigment performs, as well as in the resulting luster.

Silver carbonate is added to the earth substances to produce the yellow, gold, bronze, and sometimes other luster colors; the color produced depends largely on the glaze composition and on the firing schedule, as well as on the amount of smoking accomplished during firing. Copper carbonate is used to create red and ruby lusters, as well as a metallic, coppery luster that sometimes results. Here again, the glaze, firing schedule, and amount of smoking play an important role in the result. Bismuth trioxide usually produces a pearly iridescent luster when used with other lustering agents. A small amount of mercury sulfide seems to intensify the brilliance and color of the lusters.

Preparing Luster Pigments

To prepare your luster pigments, weigh out the proper amount of each ingredient, then place all the ingredients in a clean pan and mix them thoroughly with just enough water to wet the materials. The pigment should have a paste-like consistency, like that of artists' oil paints when squeezed from the tube, or possibly slightly more fluid. Use a rubber kidney to work the paste through a 60-mesh screen, and store it in a jar that can be tightly sealed — a small baby food jar is handy for this purpose.

Applying Luster Pigments

You will need an assortment of brushes to apply your luster pigments. The small, well-tapered Japanese brushes are excellent for this purpose. When you first start to paint on the pigments, you may find it difficult to add anything but blobs of pigment to the glaze surface, but a little practice with brushes and pigments will solve that problem.

Although the pigment need not be heavily applied, it must cover the surface to be lustered. Lines and bands may be applied by centering the piece on the wheel, and as the wheel turns, touching the tip of a fully charged brush to the surface of the piece where the line or band is desired. You may also apply the pattern using short brush-strokes, being careful to keep the brush fully charged as you paint.

If the pigment runs as you apply it, it probably contains too much water. If it goes on in lumps or bumps, it probably contains too little water. You can correct this by adding a few drops of water to the pigment in the jar and stirring with a piece of small dowel rod about 6″ or 8″ long. It is possible to correct errors on the piece using a very sharp needle point, but this must be done before the pigment is completely dry or entire sections of decoration may chip off. When decorated, let the piece dry, and it will be ready to fire.

Luster Pigment Compositions

An interesting feature of lusters is that one composition seldom yields identical results when fired more than once on exactly the same firing schedule, and there is still greater variation from one schedule to another. The following luster pigments have been tried on a variety of firing schedules, with a variety of results.

A felt pen should be used for sketching patterns on top of smoked Arabian luster glazes. Demonstration by Robert E. Johnson.

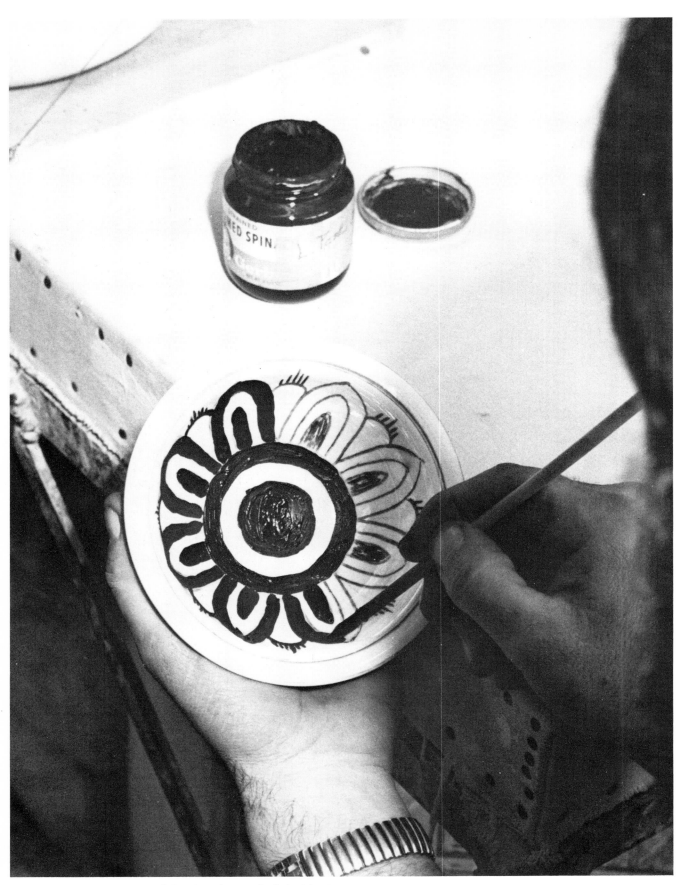

Pigment is painted on top of the glaze for smoked Arabian lusterware.

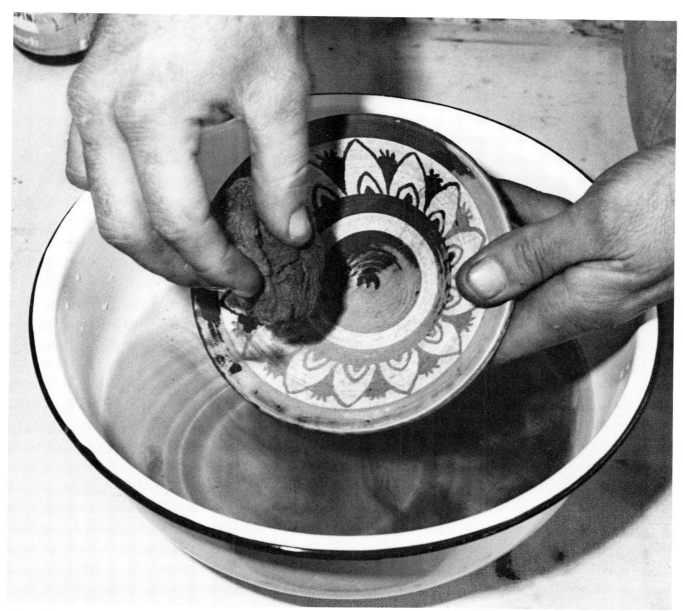

After firing, the pigment is washed off the smoked Arabian luster piece.

#2-2 Luster Pigment

Copper carbonate	50 pbw
Yellow ochre	50
Mercury sulfide	1

Note: This luster pigment always yields some variation of red. When used on glaze R.T.-12, the red has much stronger, more brilliant ruby reflections than it does on the T.A.L. glaze. On the T.A.L. glaze, the red is much more subdued, with a coppery surface quality. Also on the T.A.L. glaze, there may be strong blue and violet reflections in some firings; in other firings, there may be no reflections.

#3 Luster Pigment

Burnt umber	25 pbw
Silver carbonate	5

Note: This pigment has been consistently gold when used on the R.T.-12 glaze. It produces a flat, silvery, glossy gold when used on red clay, and a delicate yellow gold with autumn-color reflections when used on a low-firing white clay. On the transparent T.A.L. glaze, it results in a bright canary yellow.

#3-3 Luster Pigment

Burnt umber	25 pbw
Silver carbonate	10

Note: This pigment produces an antique gold with purple reflections when used on R.T.-12 glaze. On the transparent T.A.L. glaze, a light canary yellow luster results.

#3-3a Luster Pigment

Burnt umber	25 pbw
Silver carbonate	10
Mercury sulfide	1

Note: This pigment produces a flat gold with violet reflections on the R.T.-12 glaze. On the T.A.L. glaze, it produces a red-orange gold with some blue and green reflections. On the same transparent glaze, it may also result in a green luster with intense violet and gold reflections.

#4 Luster Pigment

Burnt umber	35 pbw
Copper carbonate	15
Bismuth trioxide	1

Note: This pigment produces red luster on the R.T.-12 glaze. Sometimes these lusters are a satiny red-gold; at other times, they have intense ruby and violet reflections. On the T.A.L. glaze, the pigment may be almost without visible color but with very intense violet reflections; it has also produced a very strong violet luster on this glaze.

#5 Luster Pigment

Yellow ochre	10 pbw
Silver carbonate	2
Mercury sulfide	2

Note: This pigment produces either a mottled brown and gold luster, a flat satin gold luster, or a green-gold luster on the R.T.-12 glaze. On T.A.L. glaze, it results in a very bright, dark gold and an orange luster with extremely intense red-violet reflections.

T.L. 2 Luster Pigment

Sienna	20.00 pbw
Copper carbonate	2.00
Silver carbonate	2.00
Mercury sulfide	.50

Note: This pigment consistently produces interesting variations of gold on the R.T.-12 glaze; these vary from a light, satiny gold to a brown-gold on red clay, to a definitely pink-gold on white clay. On the T.A.L. glaze, both a yellow-gold and a canary yellow luster result. For some reason, there seems to be no iridescent reflections on any of the resulting lusters.

T.L. 3 Luster Pigment

Ochre	20 pbw
Bismuth trioxide	2
Silver carbonate	2

Note: This pigment produces orangy yellow-gold on the R.T.-12 glaze. On the T.A.L. glaze, it results in a brown-gold on a black background, a definite orange-gold on a white background, and a brown-gold with intense violet reflections on a gray-tan background.

T.L. 4 Luster Pigment

Sienna	20 pbw
Bismuth trioxide	2
Copper carbonate	2
Silver carbonate	2

Note: This pigment does almost everything a luster pigment can possibly do. On the R.T.-12 glaze, it consistently results in a matte gold with intense violet reflections on a speckled white background, on a light gray background, on red clay, and on a very dark background. On the T.A.L. glaze, it produces a matte gold in combination with canary yellow and brown lusters, a purple-brown luster, a canary yellow luster, and matte gold on a black background. It is interesting that no indications of pink or red have resulted from the copper carbonate in this pigment.

The Luster Kiln

The following is a description of the kiln designed specifically for firing luster ware. It is essential that smoked Arabian luster ware be fired in this kiln, and the liquid and flash lusters discussed later in this chapter may also be fired in this kiln. A source of the plans and instructions for constructing such a kiln is listed in the Suppliers List at the back of this book; you can either build the kiln yourself or have it built for you rather inexpensively.

The kiln should be constructed of #2600 porous insulating brick, with a top opening the size of half a brick. It should have the following inside measurements: 14 5/8″ high, 13 1/4″ wide, and approximately 18″ deep. It should have four Fisher type Bunsen burners, two on each side, and an unattached brick may be used as a damper.

The plans for this kiln call for a carborundum shelf floor 1/2″ x 9 1/4″ x approximately 16″, which is raised 1/2″ above the surface of the bottom bricks, and supported by pieces of 2″ square carborundum shelf supports. There is one shelf the same size as the floor; the size of both the floor and the shelf allows for a 2″ clearance on each side between the floor and kiln wall and the shelf and kiln wall.

There is a carborundum ceiling shelf 1/2″ x 11 1/4″ x 18″, which provides a 1″ clearance on each side between the ceiling and the wall. The same kind of 2″ square carborundum shelf supports are placed along the top sides of the ceiling and act as baffles to prevent reduction materials from falling onto the ware below.

All reduction material should be wrapped in twisted newspaper packets and dropped onto the ceiling through the hole in the top of the kiln. The loose porous brick may be used to close the top during the reduction process.

To insure the necessary control of your firing, you should open the burners to their maximum capacity and control the gas supply by using a valve in the gas line that leads to the kiln. This valve should have a handle and a pointer that moves over a graduated scale. The scale should be marked off in sixteenths so that, if you wish, you can turn your kiln on to only 1/16 capacity. This choice is important, since you should fire pieces decorated with luster pigments to only somewhere between cone 022 and cone 019, and you will need complete control of the kiln. You will notice in the firing schedules later that the kiln is started with the valve turned on to 3/16 capacity. This is necessary to compensate for the reduction in gas pressure that occurs as the line to the kiln becomes longer and narrower with increased elbow turns.

Firing Smoked Arabian Lusters

Firing lusters is exactly the opposite of firing reduced copper glazes; in a luster kiln, you do want clouds of smoke, which may be produced in a number of ways. For smoked Arabian lusters, ordinary moth balls provide an almost ideal source of smoke. I say "almost" because breathing the smoke and fumes from moth balls may be harmful to you. If you use moth balls, be sure you have plenty of good ventilation — a hood over the kiln with a strong exhaust fan to the outside of the building will provide excellent ventilation. If your kiln is in an open shed or outdoor shelter where the smoke can escape into the atmosphere, no hood is necessary.

Other reducing materials such as sawdust alone or soaked in machine oil, oily rags, or small pieces of wood alone or soaked in machine oil may also be used. Whatever you use, be sure to wrap it up in small packages that can be dropped through the hole in the top of the kiln. Light the burners with the kiln door open and adjust the flame so that its tip comes 4″ up the wall, (the width of two bricks). When this procedure is followed in the kiln just described, the valve pointer indicates three-sixteenths. After the kiln is started, follow one of the firing schedules for smoked Arabian luster ware presented later in this chapter, or use them as guides in developing firing schedules for your kiln.

During the intervals of smoking the ware, expect the flames to come down around the burners outside the firing chamber. This is a natural occurrence, since the opening in the top of the kiln is covered and there is back pressure inside the kiln. Also, you may expect the gases and fumes resulting from the reduction material to burn around the outer edge of the door.

At the close of the firing procedure, make the final insertion of reduction material. Be sure to keep the kiln turned on until the last insertion has been made. If the kiln is turned off before the final charge of reduction materials has been inserted, there may be a mild explosive sound when the gases released by the material ignite. After firing is completed, let the ware cool until it can be han-

This commercially available kiln was designed especially for firing luster ware.

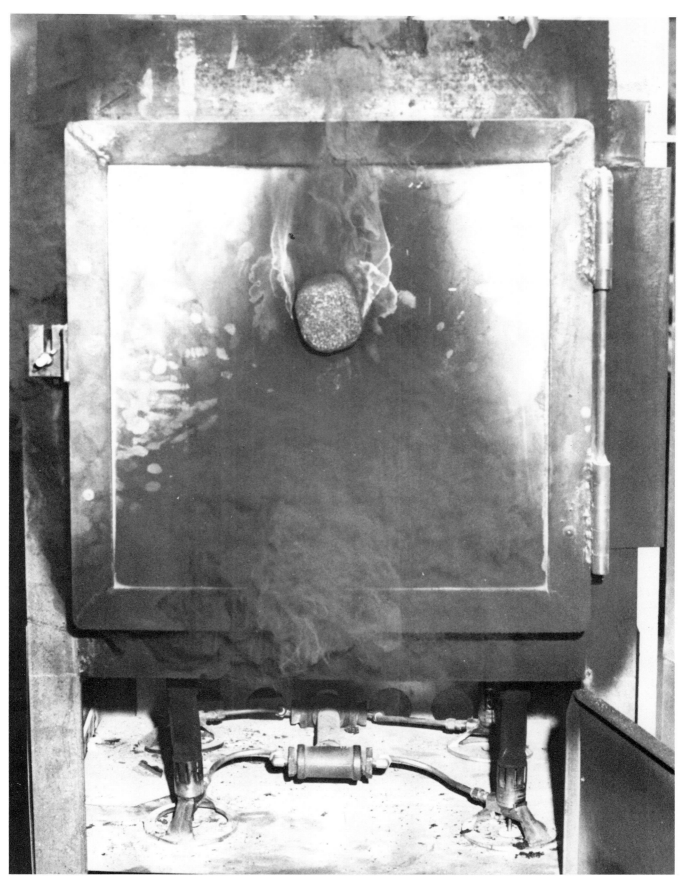

Luster ware being smoked in the luster kiln.

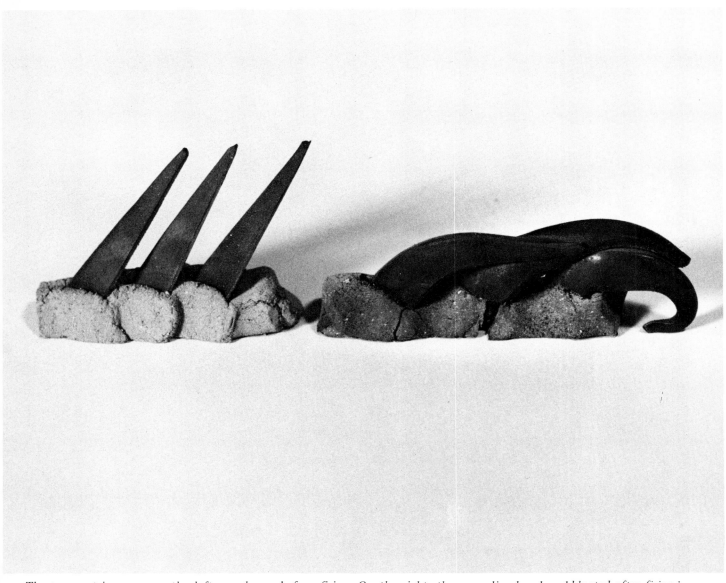

The pyrometric cones on the left are shown before firing. On the right, they are discolored and bloated after firing in a smoked Arabian luster kiln.

dled without gloves, then remove it from the kiln and wash the pigment from the surface of the glaze.

Firing Schedules for Arabian Lusters

The following firing schedules are given in detail because a variation of only a few minutes can make a great difference in the product. You will notice in these schedules that alternate periods of smoking and non-smoking are called for. The reason for this is that when the top of the kiln is closed, the temperature inside the kiln tends to drop, since at that time the flames are located primarily around the burners outside the kiln. When the top of the kiln is open during non-smoking periods, the temperature is regained. Thus it is through alternate smoking and non-smoking periods that a relatively stable temperature is maintained.

Schedule IV-2.

1. Start kiln. Tip of flame should come 4″ up kiln wall.
2. After 30 minutes, turn kiln to 3/8 on valve gauge.
3. After 35 minutes, close top, insert 4 moth balls. Kiln interior should be dull red.
4. After 5 minutes, open top.
5. After 10 minutes, close top to 7/8, insert 7 moth balls.
6. After 5 minutes, close top, insert 5 moth balls.
7. After 5 minutes, open top one-half.
8. After 5 minutes, close air intake on burners and tape intake area with masking tape.
9. After 5 minutes, close top, insert 10 moth balls.
10. After 5 minutes, insert 6 moth balls.
11. After 3 minutes, open top.
12. After 5 minutes, close top, insert 5 moth balls.
13. After 2 minutes, insert 5 moth balls.
14. After 5 minutes, insert 5 moth balls.
15. After 5 minutes, insert 10 moth balls.
16. After 7 minutes, insert 5 moth balls, then turn off kiln.

Schedule IV-3.

1. Start kiln with valve on 3/16, flame tip 4″ up wall.
2. After 30 minutes, set valve on 3/8.
3. After 35 minutes, close top, insert 4 moth balls. Kiln interior should be a dull red color.
4. After 5 minutes, open top.
5. After 10 minutes, close top 7/8, insert 7 moth balls.
6. After 5 minutes, close top, insert 5 moth balls.
7. After 5 minutes, open top one-half.

8. After 5 minutes, close air intake on burners and tape them.
9. After 5 minutes, close top, insert 10 moth balls.
10. After 5 minutes, insert 6 moth balls.
11. After 5 minutes, open top.
12. After 10 minutes, close top, insert 5 moth balls.
13. After 2 minutes, insert 5 moth balls.
14. After 5 minutes, insert 5 moth balls.
15. After 5 minutes, insert 10 moth balls.
16. After 6 minutes, insert 5 moth balls, then turn off kiln.

Schedule IV-4.

1. Light kiln, open valve 3/16.
2. After 30 minutes, open valve 3/8, close top 1/2.
3. After 45 minutes, close air intake on burners but do not tape them, close top, insert 4 moth balls. Kiln interior should be a dull red.
4. After 5 minutes, open top.
5. After 8 minutes, close top 7/8, insert 7 moth balls.
6. After 5 minutes, close top, insert 5 moth balls.
7. After 5 minutes, open top 1/4.
8. After 5 minutes, close top, insert 10 moth balls.
9. After 5 minutes, insert 6 moth balls.
10. After 3 minutes, open top 1/2.
11. After 5 minutes, close top, insert 5 moth balls.
12. After 2 minutes, insert 5 moth balls.
13. After 5 minutes, insert 5 moth balls.
14. After 5 minutes, insert 10 moth balls.
15. After 7 minutes, insert 10 moth balls, then turn off kiln.
16. After kiln has been turned off for 9 minutes, insert 10 moth balls.

Note: The final 10 moth balls, inserted after the kiln is turned off, may be omitted from the schedule since they have little effect on the results.

Firing Schedule IV-4-a

1. Light kiln, open valve 3/16.
2. After 30 minutes, open valve 3/8, close top 1/2.
3. After 55 minutes, close air intake on burners, close top, insert 4 moth balls. Kiln interior should be a dull red.
4. After 5 minutes, open top.
5. After 5 minutes, close top 7/8, insert 7 moth balls.
6. After 5 minutes, close top, insert 5 moth balls.
7. After 5 minutes, open top 1/4.
8. After 5 minutes, close top, insert 10 moth balls.

9. After 5 minutes, insert 6 moth balls.
10. After 5 minutes, open top 1/2.
11. After 3 minutes, close top, insert 5 moth balls.
12. After 2 minutes, insert 5 moth balls.
13. After 5 minutes, insert 5 moth balls.
14. After 5 minutes, insert 10 moth balls.
15. After 7 minutes, insert 10 moth balls, then turn off kiln.

Note: Cones were placed in the kiln during this firing. Cones 022, 021, and 020 were all down and were badly discolored and bloated as a result of the heavy reduction atmosphere.

Schedule IV-4b.

1. Light kiln, open value 3/16.
2. After 38 minutes, open valve 3/8, close top 1/2.
3. After 37 minutes, close air intake on burners, close top, insert 4 moth balls. Kiln interior should be a dull red.
4. After 5 minutes, open top.
5. After 5 minutes, close top 7/8, insert 7 moth balls.
6. After 5 minutes, close top, insert 5 moth balls.
7. After 5 minutes, open top 1/4.
8. After 5 minutes, close top, insert 10 moth balls.
9. After 5 minutes, insert 6 moth balls.
10. After 5 minutes, open top 1/2.
11. After 3 minutes, close top, insert 5 moth balls.
12. After 2 minutes, insert 5 moth balls.
13. After 5 minutes, insert 5 moth balls.
14. After 5 minutes, insert 10 moth balls.
15. After 7 minutes, insert 10 moth balls, then turn off kiln.

Note: This schedule has been tried only once. The reason for its use was to discover if ware fired on this schedule would develop satisfactory lusters while retaining a white and clear, unreduced transparent glaze. It is possible that various adjustments in this schedule may produce lusters on a white or non-reduced transparent glaze. However, reduction of some of the lead glazes is so attractive that you may not be interested in eliminating this quality.

On this schedule, cones 022, 021, and 020 were only slightly discolored and none were bloated or down. All glazes were free of reduced lead, and were therefore colorless, transparent, or white. When small areas of pigment were removed from the surface of the glaze, there was no luster present. The areas where the pigment had been removed were re-painted and the pieces were re-fired on schedule IV-4a-1.

Schedule IV-4a-1.

1. Light kiln, open valve slightly more than 3/16.
2. After 30 minutes, open valve slightly more than 3/8, close top 1/2.
3. After 55 minutes, close air intake on burners, close top, insert 4 moth balls. Kiln interior should be a dull red.
4. After 5 minutes, open top.
5. After 5 minutes, close top 7/8, insert 7 moth balls.
6. After 5 minutes, close top, insert 5 moth balls.
7. After 5 minutes, open top 1/4.
8. After 3 minutes, close top, insert 10 moth balls.
9. After 7 minutes, insert 6 moth balls.
10. After 5 minutes, open top 1/2.
11. After 3 minutes, close top, insert 5 moth balls.
12. After 2 minutes, insert 5 moth balls.
13. After 5 minutes, insert 5 moth balls.
14. After 5 minutes, insert 10 moth balls.
15. After 7 minutes, insert 10 moth balls, and then turn off kiln.

Note: Cone 022, 021, and 020 were discolored and bloated but none were down. All the re-fired luster ware turned out well. There was a minimum of reduced lead in the glazes.
Two additional schedules, IV-a-2 and IV-4c, vary only slightly from schedule IV-4a-1; however, they should be explained here. The complete schedules will not be presented, but their variations from schedule IV-4a-1 will be given.

In schedule IV-a-2, the time interval between Steps 2 and 3 is increased to one-and-a-half hours, and Step 13 consists of inserting 10 instead of 5 moth balls. In schedule IV-4c, the time interval between Steps 2 and 3 is increased to one hour and 45 minutes, and 10 moth balls are inserted in Step 13.

The following schedule may also be considered of major importance; it yields particularly successful pieces.

Schedule TR-2.

1. Light kiln, open valve 3/16, cover 1/2 top opening in kiln.
2. After 55 minutes, turn valve to 3/8 open.
3. After 15 minutes, close top, insert 3 moth balls. Kiln interior should be a dull red.
4. After 5 minutes, insert 4 moth balls.
5. After 5 minutes, open top.
6. After 10 minutes, close top 1/2, insert 6 moth balls.
7. After 5 minutes, close top 7/8, insert 10 moth balls.

8. After 5 minutes, open top 1/2.

9. After 5 minutes, close top 7/8, close air intake on burners, insert 4 moth balls.

10. After 5 minutes, close top, insert 5 moth balls.

11. After 5 minutes, insert 6 moth balls.

12. After 3 minutes, open top 1/2.

13. After 7 minutes, close top, insert 15 moth balls, then turn off kiln.

Note: In all schedule TR-2 firings, cones 022, 021, and 020 were down at the close of the firing cycle.

Liquid Gold Luster Technique

Following the decline in popularity of luster ware in the Mediterranean area, we find the rise of a new luster process in European countries. This consisted of firing liquid gold onto the surface of the finished glaze. Gold was first used extensively for decorating pottery at Vincennes, France, in about the middle of the 18th century. Although there was a revival of interest in luster wares in Italy, France, and Spain in the latter part of the 18th and 19th centuries, the products of this era were not comparable to those of earlier Islamic and Italian origin.

The following procedure for preparing liquid gold luster is quoted from Binns', *The Manual of Practical Potting* (see Bibliography). "Dissolve 1/2 oz. pure gold in a minimum volume of aqua regia (two parts hydrochloric acid, one part nitric acid), add four grs. of 'grain' tin, heat gently to facilitate solution. Mix 2 1/2 oz. balsam of sulphur and 1/2 pint best spirits of turpentine and heat until the balsam is completely dissolved. Add the gold-tin solution and stir the whole mass for several hours. Age for three days before use."

The solution of gold dissolved in volatile oils was then painted or sprayed onto the surface of the already fired glaze and heated to a dull red heat. The volatile oils were thus burned out, depositing the gold in a finely divided layer on the surface of the glaze.

Modern Liquid Luster Technique

Today, the use of the commercially produced liquid lusters is based on the European gold luster process and is a much simpler method for producing a lustered surface than that practiced by Moorish potters. Liquid lusters are prepared as resins of the metals that are naturally dissolved in such volatile oils as oil of lavender and oil of turpentine. The liquid is painted or sprayed onto the surface of the fired glaze, after which the piece is heated to cone 020 to 017 in an oxidizing atmosphere. Reduction is not necessary with liquid luster since the solution contains its own reducing agent in the form of volatile oil. The oil is burned out as a result of firing, leaving the finely divided metal fused to the surface of the glaze. A great variety of liquid lusters is currently available; these were very popular with china painters of 50 years ago and are becoming popular again.

Flash Luster Technique

Another type of luster technique has recently been publicized as "new," and is currently known as the "flash luster" technique. Information about this technique was first published by Franchet in his book, *La Fabrikation Industrielle des Emaux et Couleurs Céramiques* (see Bibliography). Some very interesting results can be produced by this process, which involves incorporating the metallic luster agent or agents into the glaze mixture instead of applying them separately on the finished glaze. For the serious potter, this seems to be the most appropriate process for the production of luster ware; the metal that produces the luster is introduced as an actual part of the glaze mixture, the luster results from the initial glaze firing, and the process does not require a second, or decorating, fire. The results of the process are erratic, as a specific glaze mixture seldom produces identical results in two firings even though approximately identical application and firing procedures are observed.

Body for Flash Lusters

As you develop flash lusters, you may want to try a number of clay bodies; the body of the ware does seem to influence the luster results. Jordan stoneware biscuited to maturity before glazing and Fetzer low-fire red clay produce particularly successful results. Clays containing iron seem to produce somewhat better results than the white clays, although either can be used. Blue Hill clay from Rowantrees Kilns (see Suppliers List) is also a good body for luster development. All of the red low-fire clays (cone 06 to 04) seem to give good results more consistently. Keep in mind that the clay you choose should be a smooth clay with no grog or at most a minimum of fine grog. The pieces should be biscuited to about cone 04 before glazing.

Flash Luster Glaze Compositions

The glaze composition is of primary importance in producing satisfactory flash luster effects. Fritted glazes that have a strong alkaline composition produce particularly interesting luster surfaces, and the results of raw lead glazes rank second in appeal. Some of the frits that work well are Ferro frits #3195, #3134, #3124, and #5301 (see Suppliers List).

You should apply the following glaze compositions as a medium coat.

Flash Luster Glaze #1

Ferro frit #3195	100 pbw
China clay or kaolin	5
Silver carbonate	1
Bismuth trioxide	1

Flash Luster Glaze #2

Ferro frit #3195	100 pbw
China clay or kaolin	10
Silver carbonate	2

Flash Luster Glaze #3

Ferro frit #3195	100.00 pbw
China clay or kaolin	10.00
Silver carbonate	2.00
Copper carbonate	1.00
Gold chloride	.50

Flash Luster Glaze #24

White lead	71.00
Whiting	12.50
Maine feldspar (Oxford)	41.50
Calcined kaolin	6.50
Silica	22.50
Zinc oxide	2.00
Tin oxide	12.50
Copper oxide	1.50
Cobalt oxide	8.60
Rutile	4.00

A Gold Glaze (cone 8)

White lead	62 pbw
Sodium uranate	14
Silica	18
Rutile	6

Note: In the true sense of the word, this glaze belongs in the luster category; when fired alone in the kiln, it results in a brilliant gold glaze. When 1/2 of 1% of cobalt is added to the glaze, it becomes green-gold. If a glaze containing a relatively small amount of molybdenum is fired in the kiln with this gold glaze, the molybdenum fumes cause the gold to become iridescent with red, violet, blue, and green reflections. Too much molybdenum will cause the glaze to become a matte. The fumes of a medium amount of molybdenum will produce crystals on the surface of the gold, along with iridescence. This glaze is very fluid; if applied too heavily, it will run and dissolve the brick pedestal. This in turn will cause the piece to fall to one side, and the glaze will then fuse it to any other piece it touches.

Firing Flash Lusters

Firing flash luster ware is not a complicated process; for most successful firing, a small electric kiln should be used. The small Amaco kiln from the American Art Clay Company (see Suppliers List) is ideal.

Procedure A. The kiln used for the following firing schedule was about 25 years old, but the present model, FA-44, should also work quite well.

1. Glost fire the ware to cone 06 or cone 04.
2. Cool the ware. This may take no more than 1/2 hour; rare exceptions such as luster glaze #24 should be cooled for only 15 minutes. Since this kiln has no pyrometer, the only way to determine the cooling period is to experiment with your kiln, cooling the ware to a dull red heat.
3. Reduce for at least 1 hour; in some instances, for 1 1/2 hours. Successful pieces have resulted from reducing until the kiln was completely dark inside.

Reduction Procedures. In an electric, front-loading kiln, the reduction material should be inserted through the spy hole in the door. The following are four reduction methods that work well in electric kilns.

1. Insert moth balls through the spy hole on a schedule of 5 moth balls every 6 minutes for 1 hour.
2. Insert small, lighted Bunsen burner through spy hole, use clay coil to seal around burner and door. Keep the Bunsen burner turned on full for 1 1/2 hours.
3. Insert 4″ slivers of yellow pine soaked in machine oil into the ware chamber for 1 hour.
4. Insert 5 moth balls at 5 minute intervals for the first 15 minutes. Then insert 5 moth balls at 10 minute intervals for the next 50 minutes.

Firing in a Luster Kiln

Flash lusters react quite differently than the smoked Arabian lusters when fired in the luster kiln described earlier. The following are the results obtained by firing flash luster glazes in this kiln on a variety of schedules:

Procedure for Glaze #1. Fire to cone 06 in approximately 4 hours; cool 26 minutes with the top half open; reduce by dropping 10 moth balls (in a twisted paper pouch) through the top opening every 5 minutes for 1 hour. The result is a gray-tan glaze with much violet, red, and blue iridescence. The same composition, when fired to cone 04, cooled for 47 minutes with the top half open, and reduced for 1 hour on the same schedule, results in a dark gray glaze with much violet and some gold iridescence. Variations in the length of the cooling interval and the amount of reduction create extreme variations in the resulting luster. For example, when cooled 45 minutes and reduced on the same schedule, a solid gold surface results on low-fire white clay.

Procedure for Glaze #2. Fire to cone 06 in 4 hours; cool 38 minutes with the top half open; reduce by dropping 10 moth balls through the top opening every 5 minutes for 1 hour. The result is an entirely mirrorlike silver surface on red low-fire clay. The same composition fired on white clay on the same schedule produces only a partially lustrous glaze.

Procedure for Glaze #3. Fire to cone 06 in 4 hours; cool 40 minutes; reduce by dropping 10 moth balls through the top opening every 5 minutes for 1 hour. The inside of a red clay bowl becomes dove-gray with gold, violet, and red reflections; the outside becomes matte silver. The same glaze fired on white clay on the same schedule seems to be over-reduced and displays some green, violet, and red reflections at the edge of an apparent flame flash.

Additional flash luster firings in the luster kiln have indicated that the number of shelves, shelf supports, and pieces used can make a great difference in the results. If the ware is heavily stacked, it needs a longer cooling period (as much as 55 minutes). Since the kiln which you can build yourself described earlier is relatively new, variations of the amount of reduction performed in a heavily stacked kiln have not yet been tried.

*This paddled thrown bottle
by Claude Horan
shows slip painting
and incised decoration.*

Underglaze Decoration

So far in this book, we have considered effects which result from the glaze itself, such as crystalline, copper red, and ash glazes, and effects on the surface of the fired glaze, such as lusters. There are some other glazing effects which deserve consideration. The technique for achieving each of these will be presented separately with their respective glazes.

The first technique is underglaze decoration in which underglaze pigments are applied to the biscuit after which the glaze is applied. The second technique is inlaid glaze painting where one or more glazes are inlaid in a previously applied coating of unfired glaze. The third technique involves painting the decorating pigment on top of a coating of unfired glaze, as in superimposed glaze painting or majolica. The fourth technique makes use of soluble salts solutions which are painted onto a previously applied coating of unfired glaze.

Underglaze Painting

The technique most often used in underglaze decoration is underglaze painting. The medium is commercially produced underglaze color made by calcining together various metallic oxides and other ceramic materials. You may buy the colors already prepared and ready for painting, or you may prepare your own. Underglaze painting can be done on almost any biscuited clay body, although most satisfactory results are usually achieved on a cream, white, or buff body.

Decorating Tools and Materials

For underglaze decorating, you will need a piece of glass approximately 6" x 10"; either plate or window glass will do. A selection of several powdered underglaze colors comes next, then some frit to use as a flux that you will mix with your colors. Ferro frit #3124 may be used for firing to cone 06 or above; for temperatures below cone 06, use Ferro frit #5301. A couple of watercolor brushes of different sizes should be used for painting, and a small bottle of glycerine may be used as a medium for mixing your colors.

Although you will doubtless want to expand this list, the following colors will help you get started:

1. Mason #8 U.G. Naples yellow.
2. Mason #307 U.G. golden brown.
3. Mason #301 U.G. chestnut brown.
4. Mason #19 U.G. French green.

Preparing Underglaze Decoration

The procedure for underglaze decorating is not complicated, but the color should be carefully applied. If the pigment is too thick, it may result in a blistery surface when the piece is glazed and fired. In the beginning, you may find it necessary to sketch the decorative motif on the biscuited surface first, using a soft lead pencil or a brush and water colored with vegetable dye. However, you will soon be creating spontaneous motifs without sketching them first.

Decorating Procedure

Mix three parts of color with two parts of the frit appropriate for your firing temperature. Place the mixture on the glass slab and add glycerine drop by drop. As you add the glycerine, use a palette knife to grind the mixture with a rotary motion. When enough glycerine has been added to create the consistency of oil paint, you will be ready to paint.

By thinning the color with drops of water, you can create a variety of shades; lapping brushstrokes, you can produce variations in the intensity of the color. If the painted piece must be handled very much before glazing, give it a hardening-on fire to cone 06. This fire will set the color, and the glaze may be brushed on without smudging the pattern. Finally, glaze and fire to maturity.

If you are firing decorated stoneware to cone 9, you may want to try the following transparent glaze:

Transparent Glaze (cone 9)

Custer keystone feldspar	44 pbw
Georgia china clay	13
Whiting	15
Silica	28

Inlaid Glaze Painting

Inlaid glaze painting is another technique that includes decorating with glaze. Jordan clay provides a good body for this process. Begin by first biscuit firing your piece, then soak the piece in clear water for about 1 1/2 minutes and rub it dry using a clean cloth. Apply a 1/8" coating of glaze over the entire surface; this will provide the background color for the decoration. Permit the glaze coat to dry until it will not stick to your hands, then use a soft lead pencil to freely sketch the desired decoration onto the surface of the glaze. Using a very sharp, thin needle or a sharp knife point, incise (cut through) the glaze coat along the sketched lines. Next, lay bare the area inside the incised lines by using the knife point to scrape away the glaze. After all the glaze inside the lines is removed, inlay the exposed areas with different colored glazes.

You can do this by painting successive layers of glaze into the desired areas until the new glaze is the same thickness as the background.

The following feldspathic glaze works well on Jordan clay; other material can be added to it to create a variety of colors:

Feldspathic Glaze

Custer keystone feldspar	45 pbw
Edgar plastic kaolin	15
Whiting	15
Silica	25
Titanium dioxide	10

A light green glaze results from the addition of 1.5% copper carbonate; a darker green is the result of 4% addition of copper carbonate; brown may be created by a 2% addition of manganese carbonate to the basic glaze. This glaze should be fired to cone 9, in an oxidizing fire.

Superimposed Glaze Painting (Majolica)

Superimposed glaze painting is a technique known by many names; at different times in different places it has been called majolica, faience, and delft. In America, superimposed glaze painting is known as both on-glaze painting because the decoration is applied on top of a coating of unfired glaze, and as in-glaze painting because the colored decoration soaks into the glaze coat during the firing process, thus producing an "in-glaze" decoration.

The clay for production of this type of decoration should be hard and durable but not vitreous. A good body for the ware is Fetzer red clay, which should be fired to cone 06 or 04. The glaze must be one that does not move or flow when molten, since movement of the glaze coat during the firing process distorts the decoration.

Preparing Colored Decorating Glazes

Depending on its composition, the decorating medium may be prepared in either of two ways. The first involves mixing a quantity of the glaze to be used for the coating, in powder form, with previously determined quantities of metallic coloring oxides or earth pigments. The mixture can then be stored in covered jars so that a quantity is on hand when needed. (Several glazes that are suitable for use in superimposed glaze painting are listed later on in this chapter.) The proportion of coloring oxide to glaze should be from 5% to 20% by addition, depending on the color intensity desired and the oxide used. The only sure way to determine what color will result from which coloring oxide is to experiment. In most glazes, the following quantities of oxides will produce the specified colors:

Cobalt oxide. 5% produces blue.

Manganese dioxide. 5% produces brown.

Copper oxide. 5% produces green.

Iron oxide. 5% to 20% produces yellow to brown.

Nickel oxide. 5% to 10% produces yellow-gray green.

If you use this method for preparing color, weigh out the correct proportions of glaze and coloring oxide and dry grind them together for 2 to 3 hours on the ball mill. If the materials are not thoroughly ground, you may get speckles of color instead of the full color desired.

To prepare the colored glaze for application, place a small mound about the size of a green pea on a glass slab, add glycerine or gum tragacanth solution drop by drop, and grind and mix with a palette knife until the mixture is the consistency of oil paint. The paint-like glaze can then be thinned to the desired painting consistency by adding drops of water. Mix more color and glycerine as needed.

Paint the colored glaze on top of a previously applied coating of unfired glaze that has been fixed with a coating of gum tragacanth solution.

Glazes for Superimposed Glaze Painting

You should apply a medium-thick coat of the initial glaze to the entire surface of the biscuited piece; you may apply the glaze by either dipping or spraying. After you have applied the glaze, spray the surface with a coating of gum tragacanth solution, let the piece set for 12 hours, and it will be ready for decorating. Paint on the decoration using sure, deft strokes and a Japanese long-bristle brush. As a general rule, painting over an area is not desirable; a little color goes a long way, and a second coat is not required. The following are several glazes that can be used as the initial glaze coating and then mixed with coloring oxides to produce the decoration.

R.L.M. Majolica Glaze (cones 1 – 6)

Colemanite	25 pbw
Buckingham feldspar	27
Kona A3 feldspar	28
Talc	3
Edgar plastic kaolin	8

Zircopax	11
Lithium carbonate	1
Tam rutile	1

Note: This glaze is gray-white with a slightly semi-matte texture and takes colors well. If you want the colored decoration to be somewhat broken up by circular white dots, wet grind the materials by hand in a mortar and pestle for 15 minutes and screen them through a 60-mesh screen. Apply the glaze coat about 1/16″ thick.

SF #7 Majolica Glaze (cone 06 – 02)

Ferro frit #3124	30.00 pbw
Ferro frit #3304	32.00
Edgar plastic kaolin	2.00
Custer keystone feldspar	5.00
Kona F4 feldspar	10.00
Magnesium carbonate	2.00
Zircopax	2.75
Tin oxide	10.00
Bentonite	5.00
Epsom salts	.75

Note: This glaze should be semi-matte at cone 06, more glassy at cone 02. It is a completely opaque, flat white glaze. For a creamy white color, substitute rutile for magnesium carbonate.

30 C. Majolica Glaze (cone 06 – 04)

Ferro frit #3304	65 pbw
Ferro frit #3124	80
Edgar plastic kaolin	5
Kona F4 feldspar	32
Zircopax	7
Tin oxide	20
Bentonite	15

Note: This glaze may be "pebbled" on by spraying from a distance, sprayed with gum tragacanth solution and dried, then decorated and glost fired at cone 06 or 04.

Glaze Stains for Superimposed Decoration

Powdered commercial glaze stains or underglaze colors may be used instead of metallic oxides or earth pigments as superimposed decoration. These may be prepared at the time the decoration is to be applied. The preparation of powdered color is similar to that of glazes that include oxides. The powdered color should be mixed and ground on a glass slab in an identical manner. The proportion for grinding is usually 2 parts of underglaze color or glaze stain to 3 parts of frit #3124. The following are commercial underglaze colors and glaze stains that will produce specific colors when combined with frit #3124 in the proportions just described.

Mason #8B delphinium blue. Produces blue-gray.

O. Hommel #4A 820 chocolate brown. Produces chocolate brown.

Mason #193 Alpine rose. Produces pink.

Mason #201 chestnut brown. Produces brown-black.

Mason #19 French green. Produces turquoise-green.

Mason #M medium blue. Produces violet-blue.

Mason #4-B mazarine blue. Produces purple-black.

Mason #924 deep olive green. Produces yellow-green.

Mason #2225 leather brown. Produces orange-yellow.

Mason #307 golden brown. Produces burnt orange.

Harshaw #1074 X yellow green. Produces chartreuse.

Soluble Salts Decoration

Decoration done with soluble salts may be considered a second type of in-glaze decoration. It is often used in combination with other techniques; for example, with incised lines, mishima, or slip trailing. It consists of applying water solutions of sulfates or nitrates of various color-producing metals to the piece. This may be done in two ways: by painting the solution onto the surface of the biscuited piece before applying the glaze; by painting the solution on the surface of a coating of unfired glaze. The second method produces brighter color. In either method, the subsequent firing causes the salt to be incorporated into the glaze coating, producing the color characteristic of the metal used.

Preparing Salt Solutions

Prepare the solution by dissolving the metallic salt crystals in water until a residue of undissolved crystals remains in the bottom of the container. You now have a saturated (100%) solution. If you apply this over a coating of opaque white or light-colored glaze, it will produce a pattern of intense color. If you want a lighter color, simply dilute the solution with more water; 1 part of the 100% color solution to 3 parts water will give you a 25% solution, and so on. Do not coat the glaze coating with gum solution when you use soluble salts, because it is the absorbent quality of the glaze that keeps the solution from spreading or running. The glaze compositions given for use with majolica will work well for use with soluble salts solutions.

This stoneware jar is made from a buff stoneware body containing granite grog. Red iron oxide was painted to form the pattern under a creamy textured matt glaze.

Raku Ware

Raku ware is somewhat fragile and is more decorative than useful. It was first produced in Japan by Raku-Chojiro (1515–1592). One of Japan's greatest tea masters, Sen-no-Rikyu, had a strong influence on Chojiro's development of raku. This low-fire, very soft-bodied ware, which was glazed with a lead glaze and was quite similar in style to Korean Yi dynasty tea bowls, was made exclusively for use in the tea ceremony. The raku tea bowls were glazed in three colors: black, red, and white.

Meaning of Raku

Toyotomi Hideyoshi, military ruler of Japan during that period, was so attracted by raku ware that he granted Jokei, Chojiro's son, a gold seal to be used as a signature on all his ware. The seal was engraved with the Japanese character for the word "raku," which signified "enjoyment of freedom," the highest ideal of the people at that period. The seal was actually granted in memory of Chojiro, who had produced his ware in Hideyoshi's palace. To the present time, the descendents of Jokei have continued to use the seal to mark their ware.

Today raku ware is made by many individuals and in many small factories in Japan. However, we might say that the present descendent of Jokei makes the only genuine product. In fact, the making of raku ware has become so widespread that in present-day Japan the word "raku" truly means low-fired ware with a lead glaze.

Raku Process in Japan

Today in Japan, the ware made in the raku tradition is biscuited and then glazed with a lead glaze. After glazing, the pieces — primarily red tea bowls — are rapidly fired and taken from the kiln as soon as the glaze is melted. Upon removal from the kiln, they are set aside to cool in the open air of the studio. This rapid cooling, along with the underfired body, causes the glaze to craze badly.

These conditions result in a ware that produces a soft thud, rather than a clear bell-like note or loud sound, when struck by a hard object. The soft, subdued sound that results when powdered tea is whisked in a raku bowl, is what makes raku ware so popular among tea ceremony devotees. As a whole, the red raku bowls made in Japan are very subdued in color and general character. They feel soft in the hands, and their walls are so thick that no heat, or at most only a slight warmth, is felt through them when they contain hot tea.

Black raku bowls are treated somewhat differently than other raku ware during the production process. They are fired one at a time in a very small kiln, usually below ground level. This small kiln is fired somewhat higher than the regular raku kiln. When removed from the kiln, the black bowls are plunged immediately into a bucket of cold water; if this were not done, the glaze would turn brown. The glossy black of the raku glaze is highly prized by the Japanese — thus the quick cooling procedure.

Raku Process in America

The American process for production of raku ware varies somewhat from the original Japanese process. In fact, most so-called raku ware made in America is related to the Japanese process in name only. In America, raku means a quick and rapid process for firing ware. Japanese raku ware is most often fired at a very low temperature and glazed with a lead glaze. We very often fire as high as cone 02, and we almost never use a lead glaze. However, the greatest difference between Japanese and American raku is the reduction process to which we subject our ware. We seem to feel that raku must be heavily reduced after it comes from the glaze kiln; the Japanese process involves no reduction.

The difference in the resulting product is quite marked. Japanese tea bowls are very calm, quiet, and unassuming; our raku products are very vigorous and striking, with a brilliant surface luster and strong contrasts in the crackle.

Equipment and Materials for Raku

The most important piece of equipment for raku is the kiln; second in importance is a pair of raku tongs. In the Suppliers List at the back of this book, you will find sources for kits that include the material necessary for building an inexpensive kiln, instructions for construction and firing, raku tongs, and pre-mixed raku glaze. Asbestos gloves, which are also essential, may be secured at your nearest welding supply dealer or hardware store. In addition, you will need a metal container that can be tightly closed, to be used for the reduction process. This reduction container should not be too much larger than the pieces being fired. A metal garbage can with a tight-fitting lid, or a five-gallon paint can with a tight-fitting lid, may be used.

You will also need some reducing material, which should be used to fill about half the can. Probably the most universally available reducing material is sawdust. Other materials such as rice hulls, excelsior, and even shredded newspaper may also be used. A word of caution — if you are using newspaper, be very careful. When used for reduction, newspaper seems to generate some sort of explosive gas and has been known to blow the top off a tightly closed container. If you are using sawdust, avoid the resinous woods such as yellow pine; these produce a sticky black coating that is almost impossible to remove from pots. Redwood sawdust is ideal, and any of the hardwoods or fruitwoods will provide excellent sawdust.

Bodies for Raku Ware

Any good sculpture clay can probably be used as a body for raku ware. However, most potters are of the opinion that a high-quality plastic, high-fire clay (stoneware or fire clay) with an addition of 20% to 25% grog is more desirable. Two good clay bodies that have been used most successfully are Westwood Ceramic Supply Company's "Jim Sullivan Clay" and Industrial Minerals and Chemical Company's "Sculpture Clay" (see Suppliers List). If you wish to prepare your own body, use a high-quality plastic fire clay or a high-quality plastic stoneware body and add about 20% 40-mesh grog.

Forming the Ware

If you want to work in the Japanese tradition, you will be working "tebineri," without the use of the wheel. However, if you are thoroughly American in your approach, you can use any of the techniques common to the production of ware.

Slab-built raku pieces can be very attractive and quite unusual. Sometimes, quite large thrown forms have been made by the raku process. If you are a beginner, however, you should attempt only smaller pieces until you have developed a great deal of skill in the process. If you do work with slabs or coil-built forms, be sure they are very well joined; joints are usually the weakest parts of the piece, and great care should be taken when such pieces are to be raku fired.

While some Americans are so daring or so skillful that they glaze and fire greenware, there is usually a very high percentage of loss through cracking and blow-out. It is much better to biscuit fire your ware to about cone 08 or 07 before glazing.

Raku, an Under-Fired Ware

Raku is basically an under-fired ware, which means that the body is not fired to maturity. Although porcelain and stoneware pieces biscuit-fired to maturity have been glazed in the raku manner, the results were not particularly exciting. Also, there is always a strong possibility that breakage will result from heat or cold shock when this method is used.

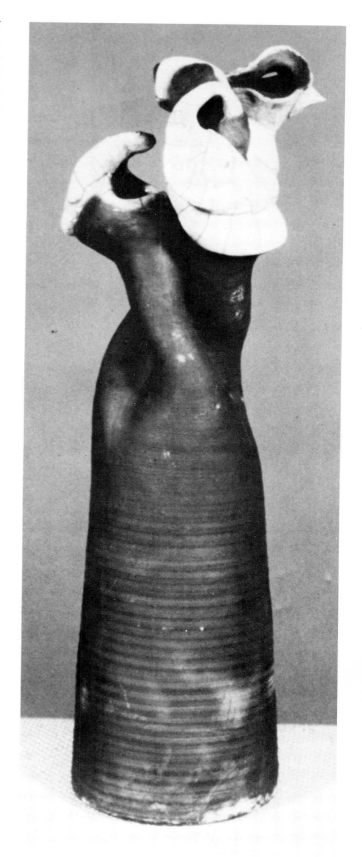

This raku vase by Shigeru Miyamoto shows a pleasing contrast of crackled glaze and an unglazed clay surface.

A slab raku weed pot by Judy Schalbarger displays a combination of glazed and unglazed surfaces.

One of the most interesting features of American raku ware is the contrast between the glazed and unglazed areas on the pot; this is particularly true when the glaze is poured or splashed onto the piece, leaving a definite pattern of glaze on the unglazed background. During the reduction process that follows the glaze firing, unglazed areas of the porous body absorb carbon from the atmosphere and consequently turn black or gray. When fired to maturity, neither porcelain nor stoneware can absorb much, if any, carbon; the body may therefore have a rather raw, unfinished appearance if fired to maturity before glazing.

Decorating Raku Ware

The appearance of raku-fired pieces is usually so strong and vigorous as a result of the process that any decoration besides the glaze is unnecessary. However, many potters do use one or several decorative processes. For example, painting or trailing colored slip on the slightly leather-hard clay produces interesting effects when the ware is then glazed and fired. A porcelain slip has been used quite successfully for this type of decoration, with and without the addition of color. If you use porcelain slip as an engobe — a coating over the entire surface of the piece — you should apply a medium-thick coating, using a wide brush or sponge, when the piece first begins to display a leather-hard texture. If you permit the piece to become too hard, the slip may peel off after the piece is glaze fired. Whenever you use slip to decorate a piece, you should allow it to dry very slowly; cover it with a plastic bag, or dry it in a closed box or container. Also, when porcelain slip is used on a piece, the results may be improved if the piece is over-fired two or three cones. To do this, leave the piece in the kiln 30 to 45 minutes after the glaze is melted.

Porcelain Slip for Raku Ware

Edgar plastic kaolin	40 pbw
Kentucky ball clay	30
Buckingham feldspar	15
Silica	15

Coloring Oxides for Porcelain Slip

The following is a list of the metallic oxides that can be used alone or in combination to produce particular colors in the porcelain slip:

Copper and Cobalt oxide. Copper oxide, 1% to 4% and cobalt oxide, .5% to 1% produce blue.

Copper oxide. 1% to 4% produces green.

Rutile or Red Iron Oxide. Rutile, 3% or red iron oxide, 2% produces cream.

Red iron oxide. 4% to 6% produces brown.

Manganese dioxide and Cobalt and Red Iron Oxide. Manganese dioxide, 4% and cobalt oxide, 3%, and red iron oxide, 3% to 5% produce black.

A lustrous surface will also result from reduction when a slip containing 10% red iron oxide and 10% copper carbonate is used under a transparent, colorless glaze. Since raku firing is done rapidly, the colors from the slips seldom run.

Luster Effects on Raku Ware

As mentioned earlier, most potters prefer the glaze and body effects achieved through the raku process without the aid of decoration. One of the most striking results of the process is the brilliant luster effect that can be achieved either by painting a thin wash of copper carbonate on the biscuit under the glaze, or by painting a thin wash of either copper carbonate or copper oxide on top of the unfired glaze coat. Copper carbonate has also been dusted onto the damp glaze coat. For dusting, use a small bag made of several thicknesses of cheesecloth. Place a tablespoon or two of copper carbonate in the bag, tie the bag closed, and shake it over the piece. The dust will sift through the cheesecloth and settle on the damp glaze coating; when dry, the piece will be ready for firing.

Applying the Glaze

In Japan, glazes are applied to raku ware only by brushing. In America, however, we use any method — brushing, dipping, pouring, or spraying — as long as the glaze coat is not so thick that it peels off the piece during firing. Keeping this danger in mind, you can create interesting contrasts on raku surfaces by varying the thickness of the glaze coating. Applying thick and thin areas of glaze on the same piece results in variations in the crackle pattern as well as in the lustrous surface. You may even want to include unglazed areas along with thick and thin areas of glaze on some of your ware.

If the glaze coat is damp when preheated, it will crack and probably crawl — gather up into bunches — when fired, or it may peel off the piece while in the kiln. After glazing, therefore, permit your ware to dry thoroughly; a day of drying is not too long.

Raku Glaze Compositions

The following are the glaze compositions most commonly used on American raku ware. For a bril-

This is a contemporary Japanese red raku tea bowl.

liant, lustrous glaze, you may also add 10% red iron oxide and 10% copper carbonate to any of the transparent glazes listed.

Raku Glaze #1

Colemanite (gerstley borate)	75%
Cornwall stone	25%

Note: A colorless, transparent glaze.

Raku Glaze #2

Colemanite (gerstley borate)	75%
Plastic vitrox	15%
Kentucky ball clay	10%

Note: A somewhat translucent glaze.

Raku Glaze #3

Colemanite (gerstley borate)	75% to 80%
Nepheline syenite	20% to 25%

Note: A transparent, colorless glaze. For a white glaze, add 8% to 10% tin oxide.

Firing Raku Ware

All raku pieces should be preheated on top of the kiln to avoid cracking. The larger the piece, the longer it will take to adjust to the heat; one and one-half hours is not too long to preheat large pieces, and very large pieces require considerably longer. As you preheat and fire your pieces, you may want to keep a record of firing times and procedures for future reference.

After you have preheated your largest pieces, put them in the kiln, replace the top of the kiln, and begin preheating your second load while you fire the first load. When the glaze on your first load of ware is melted, turn the burners down until the kiln is just burning. Then, wearing your asbestos gloves, carefully remove the lid of the kiln, leaving the preheated ware in place on top, and use raku tongs to remove the fired pieces from the kiln. Before you remove each piece, dip the tips of the tongs — which are the only area that should touch the ware — into a bucket of cold water and wipe them quickly with a dry cloth. This procedure keeps the tongs cool and prevents them from sticking to the molten glaze on the ware.

As you remove each piece from the kiln, hold it in the tongs about 30 seconds to allow the glaze to set, then place it in a reducing can half-filled with sawdust or other reducing material. Work quickly, and when all the pieces are in the reducing can, close the lid tightly so the smoke and carbon can do their work. The carbon from the burning reducing material will color the body, stain the crackle, and reduce the glaze. If you want less crackle and more luster, bury the piece completely in the reducing material; if you want more crackle with a dark stain in the crackle, place the piece on top of the reducing material.

When your first load of ware is in the reducing can, place your second, preheated, load in the kiln, replace the lid and turn the burners up so that the firing chamber will reach the maturing temperature of the glaze in about 30 to 45 minutes. Then place your third load of ware on top of the kiln for preheating.

By this time your first load of ware will have been in the reduction can for about 15 minutes and will be ready to be removed. As you remove the pieces, you may cool them by either dipping them in a bucket of water or simply setting them aside. When the pieces are cool, scrub them thoroughly to remove all excess carbon. Repeat this process until all of your ware has been fired, then replace the lid and turn off kiln.

RAKU DEMONSTRATION

The following demonstration of the raku process shows how to glaze, fire, reduce, and finish a pot in an electric top-loading kiln. Firing time is one-half to one hour.

Glaze is poured on the piece in preparation for raku firing.

The pieces are preheated on the lid of the raku kiln.

The lid of the kiln is removed, with the pieces in place on top of it.

The preheated pieces are then placed in the kiln for firing.

After the pieces are in position in the kiln and are not touching, the burner is slowly turned up.

The lid is then replaced and the burners turned higher.

The heat in the raku kiln is gradually increased until the glaze is matured.

Then the burner is turned down and the lid is removed from the kiln. Be sure to wear asbestos gloves when handling the hot lid and tongs.

The red-hot ware is removed from the kiln and swung in the air for three or four seconds to set the glaze. As soon as the glaze is set, the pieces are placed in a reduction can partly filled with excelsior and sawdust.

The red-hot ware causes the reduction material to flame up.

The lid is replaced on the can directly after the piece has been placed inside, thereby smothering the flames and causing the reduction material to smoke.

The ware is removed.

After being removed from the can, the ware is washed to clean the carbon away from the surface.

The finished piece displays a well-stained crackle.

APPENDIX

TABLE OF SODIUM SILICATES

Silicate	Formula	Weight
BW brand liquid sodium silicate	$Na_2O \cdot 1.65\ SiO_2$—E.W.	161.0
GC brand sodium silicate	$Na_2O \cdot 2.00\ SiO_2$—E.W.	182.1
K brand liquid sodium silicate	$Na_2O \cdot 3.00\ SiO_2$—E.W.	242.0
N brand liquid sodium silicate	$Na_2O \cdot 3.33\ SiO_2$—E.W.	199.8
RU brand liquid sodium silicate	$Na_2O \cdot 2.48\ SiO_2$—E.W.	210.8
Kasil #1 liquid potassium silicate	$K_2O \cdot 3.92\ SiO_2$—E.W.	329.8
SS-65 brand powdered sodium silicate	$Na_2O \cdot 3.33\ SiO_2$—E.W.	199.8

TABLE OF FRITS

Frits	Formula						
#5301	.134 K_2O	.765 Na_2O	.101 CaO	.274 Al_2O_3	.418 B_2O_3	1.72 SiO_2	1.15 F
#3110	.064 K_2O	.643 Na_2O	.293 CaO	.094 Al_2O_3	.098 B_2O_3	3.03 SiO_2	
#3124	.020 K_2O	.282 Na_2O	.698 CaO	.270 Al_2O_3	.550 B_2O_3	2.56 SiO_2	
#3134		.316 Na_2O	.684 CaO	.632 B_2O_3	1.47 SiO_2		
#P 283	.924 Na_2O	.014 CaO	.063 MgO	.20 Al_2O_3	4.37 SiO_2		
#P 239	.21 K_2O	.31 Na_2O	.48 CaO	.31 Al_2O_3	1.02 B_2O_3	2.72 SiO_2	
#P 757	.589 Na_2O .374 B_2O_3	.1 K_2O .055 SB_2O_3	.03 BaO 1.77 SiO_2	.184 CaO	.097 ZnO	.553 F_2	.201 Al_2O_3
#P-IN-72	.07 K_2O	.93 Na_2O	.09 Al_2O_3	.14 B_2O_3	2.00 SiO_2		
#P-54	.32 Na_2O	.68 CaO	.64 B_2O_3	1.47 SiO_2			
#Pb-545	1.00 PbO	.11 Al_2O_3	2.16 SiO_2				
#Pb-700	1.00 PbO	.03 Al_2O_3	1.94 SiO_2				

GLOSSARY

Alkaline. Pertaining to a soluble salt originally obtained from the ashes of plants largely sodium or potassium carbonate. In recent years lithium has been added to the group. The alkalis have a characteristic acid taste and the ability to neutralize acids and combine with them to form a salt.

Alumina. The oxide of aluminum (Al_2O_3).

Atom. The smallest particle an element can be divided into and still retain its identity as that element.

Ball Mill. A mill used for grinding ceramic materials, consisting of jars containing flint pebbles or porcelain type balls. Materials are placed in the jars with the pebbles and as the jar revolves on the mill, the materials are ground.

Boiling point. The temperature at which a ceramic glaze mixture boils when heated. All glazes have their individual boiling point.

Calcined. Having been heated to the temperature at which the chemically combined moisture is driven off.

Cc. Cubic centimeters.

Colloid. Any substance in a certain state of fine division, the colloidal state, in which the particles range in diameter from about 0.2 to about .005 micron.

Combustion. Act or instance of burning.

Cone. A pyrometric cone (pyroscope). An elongated triangular pyramid composed of ceramic materials which, when placed in a kiln with ware and subjected to heat, measures the heat work accomplished during that particular firing process. When the cone deforms, the degree of heat work which it measures is accomplished.

Contamination. The state of being impure as it applies to ceramic materials. For example, rutile is titanium dioxide with an iron contamination. $(TiO_2 + $ a small amount of $Fe_2O_3)$.

Cullet. Broken glass that can be put back in a glass furnace for re-use.

Crystalloid. A substance which forms a true solution and is capable of being crystallized.

Devitrification. To change from a vitreous to a crystalline condition. Devitrification is evident as a crystalline scum on a glassy surface.

Dunt. A glaze fault which causes the ware to crack. Dunting often results from too rapid cooling.

Excelsior. Fine, curled wood shavings.

Fluxing agent or flux. A substance that lowers the fusion point of a material.

Frit. A prefused or premelted ceramic mixture which, following fusion, is cooled, powdered, and then used as a ceramic material.

Fuming ability. The ability to smoke or throw off fumes.

Fusion point. The point (temperature) under heat at which a ceramic mixture will melt.

Ghost. Here the word is used to mean crystals which are not pronounced in contrast but are wraithlike and must be viewed at an angle to become visible.

Grog. Clay which has been formed in some manner, fired, and then pulverized.

Gum tragacanth. A gum obtained from various Asiatic or Eastern European herbs of the Pea family. The gum swells up in water and forms a molasses like solution. Used in the arts and in pharmacy.

Lawn. British pottery industry term for fine-mesh screen or sieve.

Line blend. The blend of two substances in set percentages in a straight line.

Magma. Glazes in a molten state.

Matrix. An enveloping substance of a ceramic raw

material in which the larger crystals or aggregates are embedded.

Mishima. Inlaid slip decoration.

Molecule. Atoms of elements combine to form molecules of compounds.

Opacifier. A material which remains in suspension in a glaze rendering it opaque.

Oversaturation. The most concentrated solution that can remain in the presence of an excess of the dissolved substance plus some more.

Oxidation. An oxidizing fire where more oxygen is present than is necessary for complete combustion.

Oxide. An element other than oxygen combined with oxygen.

Pbw. Parts by weight.

Red heat. The condition where refractories and any ware inside the kiln are glowing red.

Reduction. The condition inside the kiln when an insufficient amount of oxygen is present to permit all materials present to develop in their oxide form.

Refractory. A heat-resistant material. Usually in ceramics, refractory means the bricks from which the kiln is constructed as well as kiln shelves and shelf supports. At times a ceramic material or a glaze may also be spoken of as refractory.

Rubber Kidney. A flat kidney-shaped rubber tool used in ceramics.

Saggar. A refractory box in which pottery ware can be placed in a kiln to protect it from direct flame or kiln gases.

Saturation. To cause to become soaked to the point where no more can be dissolved.

Shiver (peel). A glaze fault in which the glaze breaks away from the clay body due to an excessive amount of compression in the glaze layer.

Solubility. The amount of a substance which will dissolve in a given amount of another substance.

Stabilizer. A material present or added to reduce extreme variation in the physical condition of another material or materials.

Sublimation. To pass from the solid to the gaseous state or to pass from a solid to a gaseous state and again condense to solid form without apparently liquifying. A product obtained by the process of subliming.

Suspension. The state of a solid when its particles are mixed with but undissolved in a fluid or another solid.

Translucence. The property of transmitting light without being transparent.

Triaxial blend. A tri-linear blend used to determine the percentage composition when three glazes are combined.

Vaporization. Act or process of dissipating into a vapor or the state of being vaporized.

Vitreous. Pertaining to or derived from glass therefore related to the glassy state.

Vitron. A unit of atomic structure, particularly in silica glass. Its most important property is its five-fold symmetry which precludes the formation of crystals.

Wet grind. To grind with water or some other liquid.

Willemite. Zn_2SiO_4, a mineral consisting of zinc silicate, which occurs in hexagonal prisms and in massive or granular forms.

BIBLIOGRAPHY

Baggs, A.E., and Littlefield, E., "Production and Control of Copper Red Glazes in an Oxidizing Kiln Atmosphere," *Journal of the American Ceramic Society*, XV, May 1932, p. 265.

Bentzien, Dwayne, "Copper Red Glaze Decoration of Porcelain Ceramic Forms." A project report presented to the Faculty of the Department of Art, San Jose State College, in partial fulfillment of the requirements for the MA degree, p. 12, June, 1965, California State University at San Jose library.

Binns, Charles Fergus, *The Manual of Practical Potting*, 5th ed. (London: Scott Greenwood and Son), 1922, pp. 141, 143.

Butler, A.J., *Islamic Pottery*, (London: Ernest Benn, Ltd.), 1926.

Franchet, Louis. *La Fabrikation Industrielle des Emaux et Couleures Céramiques*, Paris, 1911, p. 119.

Fraser, Harry, *Electric Kilns*, Amer. ed., (New York: Watson-Guptill), 1974.

Hobson, R.L. *A Guide to the Islamic Pottery of the Near East*. British Museum Publication, 1932. Introduction, p. 14.

Kraner, H.M., *Journal of the American Ceramic Society*, 7, 1924, pp. 868-877.

Norton, F.H., "Control of Crystalline Glazes," *Journal of the American Ceramic Society*, 20, Vol. 7, 1933, pp. 217-224.

Sanders, Herbert H., *How to Make Pottery*, 3rd ed., (New York: Watson-Guptill), 1974.

SUPPLIERS LIST

Ceramic Chemicals and Colors

Ceramic Color and Chemical Co.
P. O. Box 297
New Brighton, Pa. 15066

Ceramichrome, Inc.
Box 427
Westminster, Calif. 92683

Hammill & Gillespie, Inc.
225 Broadway
New York, N.Y. 10007

Harshaw Chemical Co.
1945 East 97th St.
Cleveland, Ohio 44106

Industrial Minerals Co.
San Carlos, Calif. 94070

Minnesota Clay
8001 Grand Ave. So.
Bloomington, Minn. 55420

Saint Joe Minerals Corp.
250 Park Ave.
New York, N.Y. 10017

Sodium Silicates

Leslie Ceramic Supplies
Small quantities:
quarts, half gallons, and gallons
1212 San Pablo Ave.
Berkeley, Calif. 94706

The Philadelphia Quartz Co.
Large quantities
1167 Public Ledger Bldg.
Philadelphia, Pa. 19106

The Philadelphia Quartz Co.
of Berkeley
Large quantities
801 Grayson St.
Berkeley, Calif. 94710

Kilns

A.D. Alpine
353 Coral Circle
El Segundo, Calif. 90245

American Art Clay Co. (Amaco)
4717 West 16th St.
Indianapolis, Ind. 46222

Cole Ceramic Laboratories
N.E. representative for A.D. Alpine
Box 248
Sharon, Conn. 06069

High Studios, Ceramic Consultant
24700 Highland Way
Los Gatos, Calif. 95030

General Ceramic Suppliers

American Art Clay Co. (Amaco)
4717 West 16th St.
Indianapolis, Ind. 46222

B.F. Drakenfeld & Co., Inc.
Washington, Pa. 15301

Fisher Scientific
Iron mortars—4 qt. size
828 Mitten Rd.
Burlingame, Calif. 94010
and 52 Fadem Rd.
Springfield, N.J. 07081
and elsewhere in the U.S.

George Fetzer Ceramic Supplies
1205 Seventeenth Ave.
Columbus, Ohio 43211

Jack D. Wolfe Co., Inc.
724–734 Meeker Ave.
Brooklyn, N.Y. 11222

Moore and Munger
33 Rector St.
New York, N.Y. 10006

Rowantree Pottery
Blue Hill, Me. 04614

Sculpture House
38 E. 30th St.
New York, N.Y. 10016

Standard Ceramic Supply Co.
P.O. Box 4435
Pittsburgh, Pa. 15205

Western Ceramic Supply Co.
1601 Howard St.
San Francisco, Calif. 94103

Westwood Ceramic Supply Co.
14400 Lomitas Ave.
City of Industry, Calif. 91744

Saggar, for holding frits, 35
Sawdust, used as reducing material, 101, 118-119
Seeding agents, 21
Setting time, for porcelain bodies, 24
Silica, 14, 21, 29, 39, 44, 45, 57-58, 65, 70
Silicon carbide, used as a reducing agent, 57-58, 67
Silver carbonate, 96
Slip: glazing, 48; trailing, 114, 121
Smoked Arabian lusterware. *See* Lusterware, smoked Arabian.
Smoking in Arabian luster kiln, 101, 105-107
Soda, 95; ash, 44, 77
Sodium: carbonate, 21; compounds, 29; glaze compositions, 27, 70
Soluble salts, 114-115
Stains, glaze, 114
Stoneware, 24, 45, 71, 73, 119, 121; reduction firing, 52
Sung Dynasty, 49, 73, 77
Superimposed glaze: painting, 113-115; stains, 114

Temmoku: compositions, 48-49; hare's fur, 46-49; oil spot, 46-49
Tin oxide, 95
Titanium: crystals, 42, 45-46; dioxide, 77; firing procedure, 46; glaze compositions, 46
Triaxial blends, 27, 43
Tungsten, 37

Underglaze decoration, 112-115; inlaid, 112-113; painting, 112; preparing, 112; tools, 112
Uranium, 37, 44

Willemite, 17

Yellow ochre, 96

Zinc orthosilicate: crystals, 17, 18, 24, 25, 42, 45, 46, 48; glaze compositions, 25
Zinc oxide, 14, 17, 18, 29, 35, 44; used for seeding crystals, 21. *See also*, Crystals.

Edited by Lois Miller and Sarah Bodine
Designed by Bob Fillie
Set in 11 point Baskerville by Harold Black Inc.
Printed and bound by Halliday Lithograph Corp.
Color printed by Sterling Lithograph